Outstanding Literacy

A Teacher's Guide to Literacy Across the Curriculum

MATILDA ROSE

Edited by M J BROMLEY

au us
books

www.booksforschool.eu

AUTUS BOOKS
England, UK

www.booksforschool.eu
Twitter: @ebooksforschool

First published in 2014

ISBN-13: 978-1500646578
ISBN-10: 1500646571

For my parents

Contents

PART ONE

INTRODUCTION

CHAPTER ONE

MAKING THE CASE FOR CROSS CURRICULAR LITERACY

Simon Sinek's book, Start With Why, explores what makes some organisations better than others. In this book, Sinek introduces the concept of the 'golden circle' which is, in fact, three concentric circles and looks like this:

Most traditional organisations, Sinek argues, work from the outside in and start with 'what?' After all, every organisation on the planet can say what it does. For example, 'we design shoes', 'we bake bread', 'we manufacture cars'. And, indeed, 'we provide an education'.

Many organisations can also say how they do what they do. In other words, they can articulate what makes them different or better than their competitors. The 'how?' is - if you like - their USP.

But very few organisations can say why they do what they do. And on this point Sinek is clear that the 'why' is not 'to make money'; turning a profit is the result of doing what they do, not the reason they do it. The 'why' is the core belief or conviction that drives an organisation; it is their *raison d'être*.

Sinek proffers two examples by way of illustration.

Microsoft, he says, works from the outside in, it starts with 'what?'. Microsoft starts by saying that it makes computer software. How? By ensuring that it is beautifully-designed and easy-to-use. For Microsoft, Sinek argues, that is where the thinking process ends.

Apple, by contrast, works from the inside out - it starts with 'why?'. It says that in everything it does it believes in challenging the status quo. How? By ensuring that its products are beautifully-designed and easy-to-use. What? It happens to make computers and phones.

At this stage, you too may be driven to ask 'why?': Why are you telling us this, woman? We bought a book about literacy and you're droning on about computer software manufacturers. Fair point. But I happen to think Sinek's golden circle is a useful mantra when leading change in schools. Rather than starting with 'what?' - what do we want teachers to do differently in the classroom - we should start with 'why?' - why do we want to change the way teachers operate? This is more than simply having a vision statement, although this is certainly a start. It is about placing the needs of students firmly centre-stage, ensuring that decisions are only ever taken in the best interests of students' wellbeing and learning, and ensuring that change is never enacted for change's sake or simply because a school leader has assumed a new responsibility and wants to make his or her mark.

In terms of literacy across the curriculum, it's particularly important we start with 'why?' because the most common barrier we face as literacy leaders is the teacher's age-old refrain, 'Why should I teach literacy? I'm not an English teacher'; a refrain which has echoed down the years. As early as 1922, George Sampson (in 'English for the English: A Chapter on National Education' published by Cambridge University Press) said "teachers always seem to think that it is always some other person's work to look after English. But every teacher is a teacher *of* English because every teacher is a teacher *in* English." Just re-read that last sentence. Wonderful, isn't it? Indeed, Sampson argued that the line "every teacher is a teacher of English" should be "written in letters of gold over every school doorway". I haven't the resources nor the influence to build this lasting memorial to George Sampson but I have asked that his magnificent words feature on the front cover of this book - in gold no less. Flick to the cover now to see what level of influence I have with my publishers.

CHAPTER TWO

THE 'WHY?'

So why does literacy matter? Why should every teacher be a teacher of literacy?

The case for promoting literacy is particularly urgent at the moment because too many students leave school without the confident and secure literacy skills they need in order to survive - let alone thrive - as adults.

Apologies in advance but I'm going to quote some depressing statistics. I don't believe in denigrating teachers nor in disparaging our education system. Teachers work incredibly hard (I know, I am one) and are, to a man (and a woman), committed professionals. As I will state later, teachers and schools are not to blame for the situation I am about to describe, but they are responsible for doing something to address it and so they need to be aware of and act on these somewhat damning figures...

In January 2012, the National Literacy Trust found that one in every six adults struggles with literacy and has a literacy level below that expected of an eleven-year-old.

Seven million adults in England cannot locate the page reference for plumbers in the Yellow Pages and 1 in 16 adults cannot identify a concert venue on a poster that contains the name of the band, the price, the date and time, and - one would imagine rather helpfully - the venue. More than half of British motorists, meanwhile, cannot interpret road signs properly. Judging by the number of points on my licence, I suspect I am one of them.

In 2009 a Department for Education (then known as the Department of Children, Schools, and Families) survey found that only 33% of students who were known to be eligible for free school meals (FSM) achieved a C grade or higher in English, as compared with 62% of non-FSM students.

The same DfE survey also found that there was a 32% gap between the proportion of students from areas of greatest deprivation who achieved a Level 5 at the end of Key Stage 3 and the proportion of students from areas of least deprivation.

A survey of 566 employers, undertaken by the Confederation of British Industry in 2011, highlighted the dissatisfaction felt by more than 4 in every 10 employers about the low standards of basic literacy demonstrated by many school and college leavers.

Teachers are not to blame, or at least not entirely. The All Party Parliamentary Group on Education reported in 2012 that literacy was a huge issue for the nation, our society and our economy, not just for schools.

The importance of improving literacy has also been recognised by governments from across Europe. A recent European Union report, for example, spoke of a 'literacy crisis that affects every country in Europe':

"If smart growth is about knowledge and innovation, investment in literacy skills is a prerequisite for achieving such growth... Our world is dominated by the written word, both online and in print. This means we can only contribute and participate actively if we can read and write sufficiently well. But, each year, hundreds of thousands of children start their secondary school two years behind in reading; some leave even further behind their peers... Literacy is about people's ability to function in society as private individuals, active citizens, employees or parents... Literacy is about people's self-esteem, their interaction with others, their health and employability. Ultimately, literacy is about whether a society is fit for the future."

If literacy is about whether a society is fit for the future, improving standards of literacy is clearly a matter for all of society not just for teachers. But teachers must play their part. And if literacy is about people's ability to function in society, improving literacy is clearly a matter for all teachers not just for the teachers of English.

In 2010 the National Literacy Trust published a report called Literacy: State of the Nation, A Picture of Literacy in the UK Today in which it reported that 92% of the British public considered literacy to be vital to the economy and essential to getting a good job. The report found that parents were the most important role models for their children. 71% of young people said that their mothers were the most important role model for reading whilst 62% cited their fathers.

Yes, literacy is a matter for society and parents clearly have a vital role to play. And so...

I say again that teachers are not to blame for the dire situation in which many people find themselves. But they share a responsibility for doing something about it and are arguably best placed to make the biggest difference. A real and lasting difference can only be made, however, if all teachers - not just teachers of English - take responsibility for developing students' literacy skills.

If your colleagues need further persuasion that literacy is important and, perhaps more crucially, that literacy is their responsibility then take a look at the latest Ofsted framework. If you cut the framework open it has the word LITERACY written right through it like the letters in a stick of seaside rock...

According to the inspection schedule, an outstanding school is one in which "all pupils have high levels of literacy appropriate to their age" and "read widely and often across all subjects". An outstanding school is also a school in which "pupils develop and apply a wide range of skills to great effect, in reading, writing and communication". Teaching of reading, writing, and communication in outstanding schools is "highly effective and cohesively planned and implemented across the curriculum". And "excellent policies [in outstanding schools] ensure that pupils have high levels of literacy" or that "pupils are making excellent progress in literacy".

And that's not all. Literacy is now built into four of the five key judgment areas - overall effectiveness; achievement; the quality of teaching; and leadership and management - that are reported on during a school inspection.

As well as being integral to the Ofsted framework, and therefore key to a school's success, literacy also features in the national Teaching Standards, a set of professional competences that all teachers are required to fulfil. These standards must feature in performance management documentation and are now central to many schools' performance-related pay procedures.

The Teaching Standards, which set the benchmark for the evaluation of teaching by school leaders and by Ofsted - require teachers to "demonstrate an understanding of and take responsibility for promoting high standards of literacy, articulacy and the correct use of standard English, whatever their specialist subject".

It is, it would follow, the responsibility of school leaders (including leaders of literacy) to check that teachers have that understanding, to establish training programmes when needed, and to monitor rigorously how effectively teachers are developing students' literacy skills as an integral element of their wider learning.

In short, if a teacher wishes to be judged good or outstanding by Ofsted, wishes to meet their performance management objectives and get a pay rise every year, s/he must embed the teaching of literacy in his/her everyday practice.

An Ofsted report called Removing Barriers to Literacy is also well worth reading if you're in search of ammunition. The report concludes that "teachers in a secondary school need to understand that literacy is a key issue regardless of the subject taught". It goes on to say that literacy is an important element of [teachers'] effectiveness as a subject teacher.

Removing Barriers to Literacy explains why literacy is important. It argues that literacy supports learning because "pupils need vocabulary, expression and organisational control to cope with the cognitive demands of all subjects". It argues that writing helps pupils to "sustain and order thought", that "better literacy leads to improved self-esteem, motivation and behaviour", and that literacy "allows pupils to learn independently" and is therefore "empowering". Moreover, it argues that "better literacy raises pupils' attainment in all subjects".

Ofsted's excellent report, Moving English Forward, which I would again recommend you read in its entirety, has this to say about literacy across the curriculum:

"Schools need a coherent policy on developing literacy in all subjects if standards of reading and writing are to be improved. Even with effective teaching in English lessons, progress will be limited if this good practice is not consolidated in the 26 out of 30 lessons each week in a secondary school that are typically lessons other than English or the 70% or so of lessons in primary schools that do not focus on English. This debate is, of course, long established and formed a central point of the Bullock report on English published in 1975. Previous efforts to raise literacy as a whole-school initiative have tended at best to have a short-term impact. The All-Party Parliamentary Group for Education recently reported that "schools should be developing cross-departmental strategies to develop literacy" and recommended that Ofsted should look "more closely at this."

- Moving English Forward (2012)

In conclusion, every teacher is a teacher of literacy. As a teacher of, say, Science, you have a responsibility to help your students learn about science, but you also have a responsibility to help them speak, read and write like a scientist. This means you have to possess some specialist knowledge of – for example - the conventions of scientific report-writing and of the ways scientists themselves write about science. But, perhaps more importantly, it means having an analytical self awareness, which enables you to identify how you speak, read and write about science so that those skills can be made explicit for your students. And this is best done by explaining, demonstrating, modelling, teaching, and giving feedback...on which more later.

So that's the WHY: why literacy is important and why it should be the responsibility of all teachers as well as society. Let's now turn our attentions to the HOW...

CHAPTER THREE

THE 'HOW?'

In this section we'll look at *how* we can promote literacy learning across the curriculum.

In April 2013, Ofsted published a paper called Improving Literacy in Secondary Schools: A Shared Responsibility which outlined seven case studies of outstanding practice in literacy across the curriculum. The report ended with this quote from Y Kassam's 1994 paper 'Who benefits from illiteracy?':

> "To be literate is to gain a voice and to participate meaningfully and assertively in decisions that affect one's life. To be literate is to gain self-confidence. To be literate is to become self-assertive. Literacy enables people to read their own world and to write their own history. Literacy provides access to written knowledge and knowledge is power. In a nutshell, literacy empowers."

> *- Kassam, (1994)*

The Ofsted report argues that achieving success in promoting literacy does not require extravagant or exotic strategies, it simply requires the following (which I have taken the liberty to paraphrase):

- For all teachers to be involved
- For all teachers to use language to promote learning in their subjects
- For the specific reading, writing, and speaking and listening needs of students to be identified
- For there to be strong links between school and home
- For the school to make clear the integral link between language and learning and effective teaching in all subjects.

And **how** can schools achieve this? Let's take a look at some aspects of good practice inspired by Ofsted's report...

I

EXAMPLES OF GOOD PRACTICE

1. Putting literacy centre-stage

Literacy needs to be seen as an integral part of teaching and learning. In order to highlight this, you could cease calling it literacy, redefining it as 'language for learning'. This move might help divorce literacy from the domain of English teachers and might place it firmly in the mainstream of teaching and learning. Literacy needs to be on the agenda whenever teaching and learning is discussed. All teachers need to ask 'How can I use language for learning effectively to improve achievement in my subject?

2. Rome wasn't built in a day

Literacy needs to become a permanent feature of your school's development plan. Literacy should not be addressed through a one-off training day or by displaying key words around classrooms; it has to become an integral part of your longer-term school improvement agenda and should inform the content of development plans in each subject. This should involve governors and may became a performance management target for teachers.

In short, there is no 'quick fix' with literacy. Instead, there needs to be a set of clear aims and a genuine commitment from all staff - including the support of the headteacher and senior team - as well as a sense of urgency.

Ofted's 'Improving Literacy' report illustrates the importance of active leadership by headteachers and other senior leaders in making the case for literacy. In the schools Ofsted surveyed, they found that headteachers cared about literacy and ensured that it remained a constant topic of discussion. They modelled the importance of literacy in different ways, of course: some personally trained older students to be literacy tutors; others taught literacy intervention classes.

As a result of this, the staff in the survey schools knew that literacy was something of importance to the school leadership team: it was evident in everything the headteacher and other senior leaders did and said; it was central to the school's vision and its improvement planning.

3. What's in it for me?

Have you ever wondered why all those people down the pub who complain that teachers have it easy - with the long holidays and the gold-plated pensions - don't re-train as teachers? If this were true, surely they'd want to hook their carriage to the easy train? But they don't. They carry on doing whatever it is they do when they're not moaning about commie teachers. Why? Because they know, beneath the bravado, that teaching is a tough job that requires a large dose of mental and physical strength and offers little semblance of a work life balance. Accordingly, as a leader of literacy, you should remember that, like you, your colleagues are busy, hard-working people with challenges of their own.

You should not assume that all teachers will welcome your cross-curricular literacy initiatives. Instead, as we explored in part one, you need to make clear and explicit the link between literacy and more effective learning in every subject.

Your starting point should be to ask every teacher what literacy skills the students in their subject need and what approaches to literacy learning will help them to become a more effective teacher of their subject. You will need to consider the different forms and purposes of reading and writing in each subject and tailor your approach accordingly. For example, writing will look very different in History than it does in Science and Maths.

4. To be or not to be an English teacher?

I'm undecided about whether or not English teachers make the best leaders of literacy. English teachers undoubtedly have the right expertise because they are the specialists in, amongst other things, language usage, spelling, punctuation and grammar. But there is a danger that any literacy initiative put forward by an English teacher will be seen as an example of English teachers asking other people to do their jobs for them. Teachers of other subjects are more likely to be seen as promoting a cross-curricular concern and may better understand the role of literacy in other subjects.

My ambivalence is heightened by the fact that, as an English teacher, I was a Literacy Coordinator, and later I appointed a History teacher as my successor. What worked in the latter case, was that he had language skills because his specialism was an essay-based subject but he could also address literacy from the point of view of a non-English teacher, focusing on what aspects of cross-curricular literacy his students needed rather than starting with the English syllabus. However, and this is not criticism of someone who was an excellent colleague and highly skilled teacher, I doubt it would have worked had he not been line managed and therefore supported by an English teacher who could help and advise along the way.

Whatever decision you or your headteacher take, it's vital that any literacy initiative you launch is seen as addressing a whole-school priority rather than assisting the English department. Literacy and English need to be divorced from each other as much as possible and the leader of literacy needs to be focused on cross-curricular literacy not on developing literacy through English.

For this reason, I'd argue that the Literacy Coordinator should report to a member of the senior leadership team (ideally the headteacher) rather than the Head of English.

In the most successful schools that Ofsted surveyed in 2013, they found that good use was made of specialists from English but that teachers of other subjects (and don't forget that teachers of Modern Foreign Languages have fantastic language expertise, too, of course) supported the development of effective literacy strategies. You'll need to provide time and resources, therefore, to encourage close collaboration between all teachers in the development of practical strategies and schemes of work.

5. Learn to share

Sharing good practice across all subjects is the key to success in raising standards of literacy in your school. It's also a great way of highlighting and celebrating the various forms of literacy that already exist in your school which, in turn, will help you to win over hearts and minds. For example, teachers of PE are likely to plan and facilitate effective class discussions and group work. By highlighting this you are showing your colleagues in PE that literacy does apply to them and that they are already doing it well. By sharing this good practice with other subject areas, you are also helping others to develop effective strategies for discussion and group work - but, crucially, these strategies are not handed down to them by the leader of literacy in the form of a decree. If good practice comes from other teachers who are using these strategies in their daily teaching practice rather than in the form of a policy document from a school leader, it is more likely to be welcomed and adopted by others.

6. The best laid schemes...

Cross-curricular literacy needs to run deeper than simply sharing some teaching strategies, however. And it must be more than an occasional token activity such as sharing key words or marking spelling. It is one thing to identify an opportunity for a piece of extended writing in a particular subject, but this isn't enough. This needs to be extended across all subjects and embedded in every scheme of work. This requires departments to reach an agreement about the teaching of writing in their subject.

You need to encourage all your teachers to design and deliver subject-specific activities that develop students' reading, writing, and speaking and listening which does not have 'improving literacy' as their learning objective. You need to create a culture and a structure in which it is normal practice for teachers to know about the good practice going on in their own school and for them to recognise how this might be translated into activities in their own subjects.

7. Libraries gave us power...

The school library and the librarian should have an important role in developing reading. Ideally, the librarian should be a part of the school's leadership structure so that they are afforded the opportunity to influence the literacy debate and to enhance the library's contribution to students' progress. Most of the imaginative programmes to encourage reading that inspectors reported in their 2013 report were inspired by a good librarian.

8. ...paved with good intentions

'Doing' more is simply not enough. For example, the fact that there is more extended writing going on in the school does not in itself ensure that the quality of writing is any better.

Imaginative initiatives might look good on an action plan and your CV but they mean nothing if they don't lead to genuine and sustained improvements. Accordingly, you need to be clear about the impact of your initiatives on student outcomes, as well as whether or not the initiatives represent good value for money and a good use of resources (including staffing).

Ofsted suggest that setting aside twenty minutes every day for reading would beg the following questions:

- Are all groups of students engaged?
- What about the poor reader who sits and pretends to read?
- What about the keen reader who reads for hours outside school?
- What about the teacher who is not a keen reader and remains uncommitted to the idea?

9. One size does not fit all

Each school is likely to face the challenge of improving literacy in a different way, a way borne out of its unique context. And this is only right - each school is different, after all.

What is true of all schools, however, is that the way to improve literacy is not extravagant or exotic; it is simple and it is concerned with fundamentals. For example, each school should:

- involve all teachers and demonstrate how they are all engaged in using language to promote learning in their subject
- identify the particular needs of all students in reading, writing, speaking and listening
- make strong links between school and home
- plan for the longer term, emphasising the integral relationship between language for learning and effective teaching in all subjects.

II

USEFUL DOCUMENTATION

Literacy should feature in every one of the school's self-assessment and planning documents including: the SEF; the school improvement plan; subject-specific improvement plans; teaching policies and procedures. In addition, it's wise to produce a list of what you've done in order to address them as well as what you plan to do in the future. A dedicated literacy improvement plan is also useful, particularly if it is a working document, regularly annotated (RAG-ed or given a percentage for the proportion of actions which have already been completed). Finally, a short position statement - updated regularly - is helpful for the purposes of inspection. Your position statement will be the key document given to inspectors to help shape their judgments so it should distil succinctly and clearly your key points and refer to other documentation where more detailed evidence can be found. It should be kept up-to-date and it should be shared widely with staff and governors.

Your position statement might be organised around the following headings:

1. Current position

2. If 'good' why and why it is not yet 'outstanding'; if 'requiring improvement' why and why it is not 'good' and so on

3. Strengths and evidence

4. Areas for improvement and evidence

5. Actions already taken to address these areas for improvement

6. Impact of these actions to date

7. Future plans / further actions to be taken

8. How you're communicating with and involving key stakeholders (e.g. a link governor, school leaders, teaching and support staff, students, parents, etc.)

Literacy policy

Your literacy policy should be short and simple. If it's long and complex, although it might impress your headteacher and chair of governors, most people won't bother to read it.

Your policy should be practical and relevant, not too academic and theoretical. It might start with a statement of intent, setting out what literacy learning should be like. Here's an example from a policy I wrote many years ago (I'm sure I was influenced by other policies and texts so make no claims of originality). I proffer this merely as an example not as a model of excellence...

Literacy learning should:
- be enjoyable, motivating and challenging;
- be actively engaging;
- be focused and led by progressive learning objectives;
- activate prior learning, secure understanding and provide opportunities to apply skills;
- meet the needs of all learners;
- develop learners' functional and personal learning and thinking skills;
- use assessment for learning to engage students.

Next, you might define what literacy means in practice, using the three domains of literacy which will feature throughout this book: speaking and literacy (or oracy); reading; and writing...

Speaking and listening is about developing the ability to:
- Listen and respond to others (adding to or arguing against);
- Speak and present (with increasing formality);
- Participate in group discussion and interaction;
- Engage in drama, role-play and performance.

Reading is about developing the ability to:
- Decode increasingly complex and challenging words across the curriculum;
- Read for meaning (through the use of reading strategies such as prediction, skimming, scanning, inference, summarising, etc.);
- Understand the author's craft (analysing the effect of the use of features of form, structure and language);
- Read and engage with a wide variety of texts;
- Research for a wide range of purposes.

Writing is about developing the ability to:
- Generate, plan and draft ideas for composition;
- Select, shape and construct language for expression and effect in composition;
- Proof-read and redraft written work, drawing on conventions

and structures;
- Use accurate grammar, punctuation and spelling;

Next, you might articulate the models of teaching that are required in order to teach literacy and language... These might include:
- direct teaching to help students acquire new skills and procedures;
- cognitive teaching and learning to help students understand new concepts and think creatively;
- social teaching and learning such as paired, group and guided learning in which students construct new knowledge for themselves through collaboration.

Finally, you might set out the skills and techniques required of literacy and language teaching which might include the following:
- activating prior knowledge (to build on what students already know);
- modelling (to make explicit language conventions and processes);
- scaffolding (to support students' first attempts and build confidence);
- explanation (to clarify and exemplify the best ways of working);
- questioning (to probe, draw out and extend students' thinking);
- exploration (to encourage critical thinking);
- investigation (to encourage enquiry and self-help);
- discussion and dialogue (to shape and challenge developing ideas);
- assessment for learning (to help students identify their own and each other's progress and plan their next steps).

Once you've written your policy - which you should do in consultation with colleagues - you might attempt to map some common literacy skills to subjects across the curriculum. Here are some suggestions...

Developing clear and appropriate expression:
Geography, Art, Science, Design and Technology, and Citizenship

Structuring and organising writing:
History, Geography, MFL, RE, and Citizenship

Using writing as a tool for thought:
All subjects

Reading for meaning:
RE, Maths, MFL, History, Science, and ICT

Developing research and study skills:
History, Geography, Design and Technology, Music, Art, ICT, and Citizenship

Active listening to understand; using talk to clarify and present ideas; and talking and thinking together:
Maths, Science, ICT, History, Geography, RE, Citizenship, Art, Music, PE, and Design and Technology

Once you've agreed your policy and have mapped literacy skills across the curriculum, you might wish to audit your current position. Conducting an audit is a good starting point because it will identify your strengths and areas for improvement (which can then inform your development plan) and it will provide a baseline assessment from which you can judge the effectiveness of your future actions.

Here are some key questions you could ask as part of your audit:

1. Are key terms and vocabulary clear and explored with students to ensure that they recognise and understand them? Are they related to similar words or the root from which they are derived?

2. Do teachers identify any particular features of key terms and help students with strategies for remembering how to spell them or why they might be capitalised (e.g. 'Parliament' in

History or PSHCE)?

3. Do teachers remind students of important core skills – for example how to skim a text to extract the main elements of its content quickly or to scan a text for information about a key word or topic?

4. Do teachers make expectations clear before students begin a task – for example on the conventions of layout in a formal letter or on the main features of writing persuasively?

5. Do teachers reinforce the importance of accuracy in spoken or written language – for example, emphasising the need for correct sentence punctuation in one-sentence answers or correcting 'we was...' in students' speech?

6. Do teachers identify when it is important to use standard English and when other registers or dialects may be used – for example, in a formal examination answer and when recreating dialogue as part of narrative writing?

7. Do teachers help students with key elements of literacy as they support them in lessons? Do they point out spelling, grammar or punctuation issues as they look at work around the class?

8. Does teachers' marking support key literacy points? For example, are key subject terms always checked for correct spelling? Is sentence punctuation always corrected?

You might also wish to focus your audit on the areas of concern Ofsted most often identifies and reports on. These are the aspects of literacy teaching that prevent schools from achieving a good or outstanding judgment and are therefore useful starting points.

Ofsted often cites the following areas of concern:
-   Transition between Key Stages 2 and 3.
-   Lack of thought around ways of encouraging a love of reading.
-   A focus on a narrow range of test or examination skills.

- Too little attention on spelling and handwriting.
- Insufficient opportunity to develop independent learning.
- Gaps between girls' and boys' achievement, especially in writing.
- Poor performance by students eligible for free school meals.
- Planning that is detailed and lacks flexibility and focuses on the learning outcomes.
- Too fast a pace with a constrained use of time.
- Too many activities, with teachers feeling they need to leap from one to another.
- Over-detailed and bureaucratic lesson plans.
- Inflexible approaches to planning lessons.
- Limited time for students to work independently.
- Constant review of learning at the expense of time spent on learning.

III

THE BIG 'O'

I promise I shan't talk about Ofsted throughout this book but permit me to linger a while longer on the Big 'O' as we consider how our almighty inspectorate defines outstanding practice in leading and teaching literacy across the curriculum…

The inspection framework says that inspectors should focus on how effectively "leadership and management at all levels enable pupils to overcome specific barriers to learning and promote improvements for all pupils and groups of pupils in the context of the individual school". It says it will judge "how relentlessly leaders, managers and the governors pursue a vision for excellence" by looking at, amongst other things:
- Improvement plans
- Policies and procedures
- Monitoring and evaluation documents

Ofsted also says it will assess how well a school actively seeks out and models best practice in literacy teaching, how it develops its staff's literacy skills, and how it tackles underperformance.

If you analyse the grade descriptors, certain key phrases stand out, and may be worth including in your own self-evaluation… but only if you can demonstrate how you do each of these things:
- Communicate high expectations and ambition
- Model good practice
- Monitor, improve and support teaching
- Plan actions based on accurate self-evaluation
- Plan a well-organised, imaginative and effective curriculum which provides opportunities for learning for all students
- Promote positive behaviour
- Offer a broad range of experiences
- Work well with parents and carers

I said earlier that literacy features in all bar one of Ofsted's key judgment areas. Let's take a look at two judgment areas and see how Ofsted define good and outstanding performance…

The achievement of pupils:
'Good' performance in this area is described as being when students "develop and apply a range of skills well, including reading, writing, communication and maths skills across the curriculum…" 'Outstanding' performance meanwhile, is when students "develop and apply a wide range of skills to great effect, including reading, writing, communication and maths skills across the curriculum…"

The quality of teaching:
'Good' performance is when "teaching…allows [students] to develop a range of skills, including communication, reading and writing, and maths, across the curriculum…" whereas 'outstanding' performance is when "every opportunity is taken to successfully develop crucial skills, including being able to use their literacy and numeracy skills in other subjects."

The inspection handbook that tells inspectors how to carry out an inspection, offers some guidance on how inspectors should collect evidence in order to reach the above judgments. They should, for example, investigate students' books to analyse how errors are reviewed and how progress is shown over time. They should ask students how they know what their next step is, how they are supported to improve, and how often teachers refer to literacy skills or targets in other subjects. They should look at marking across the school and ask whether or not it supports key literacy points. They should consider the difference between the quality of 'everyday' writing and that done under 'controlled situations'.

In gathering such evidence, inspectors are encouraged to judge whether or not there are any missed opportunities to embed key skills, whether or not all teachers mark for literacy across the curriculum, and whether or not there is evidence of progress of literacy skills in other subjects.

The best way to prepare for inspection is to carry out your own investigations, gathering evidence and questioning the impact of your initiatives. For example, you might conduct a book scrutiny in order to assess long-term progress in literacy skills across the curriculum. You might conduct a student voice survey or a series of interviews, asking the same questions Ofsted will. You might investigate expectations of marking which reference literacy in all subjects.

How do inspectors gather evidence when they inspect literacy?

Before going forth and gathering your evidence, consider what inspectors will do so that you can pre-empt them.

At Key Stage 1, the focus of inspection is on the teaching and learning of phonics so that young students have the skills they need to be able to de-code words effectively. Teaching phonics is a means to an end, not an end in itself and where students are reaching age-related expectations, Ofsted say they will not investigate in depth the teaching of phonics. However, for those children who are not reaching age-related expectations, there will be a requirement that they are being taught systematic, synthetic phonics in order to be able to de-code words. Inspectors will want to see evidence of this. In particular, inspectors will want to see evidence that the following elements of the phonics programme are being taught:

1.   Grapheme-phoneme correspondences in a clearly defined, incremental sequence

2.   The synthesis, or blending, of phonemes in order all through a word, to enable the word to be read

3.   The segmenting of words into their constituent phonemes, for spelling

4.   The understanding that blending and segmenting are reversible processes

In arriving at a judgment for 'achievement', inspectors will investigate whether or not there are any gaps in reading achievement and attainment between different groups of students. If there is a gap, inspectors will want to know what the school is doing to close the gaps and will expect tangible evidence of this. Inspectors will also want to know what proportion of students did not gain Level 4 or above in their reading by the end of Key Stage 2 and whether or not that proportion is decreasing year by year.

In arriving at a judgment for 'quality of teaching', inspectors will investigate the extent to which - and how successfully - teachers in the Early Years and Foundation Stage (EYFS) develop students' spoken language, extend their vocabulary, and familiarise them with books. They will want to know about the quality of teaching of students who are failing to make sufficient progress both in mainstream lessons and in intervention work.

In arriving at a judgment for 'leadership and management;, inspectors will investigate the extent to which the headteacher engages in the provision for reading. Inspectors will also want to know what steps have been taken by leaders and managers in order to ensure consistency in the teaching of reading.

And in arriving at a judgment for 'behaviour and safety', inspectors will investigate the extent to which any unsatisfactory behaviour is attributable to students struggling to learn to read.

Inspectors will investigate how successfully a school achieves its aim of ensuring that, by the end of Year 1, students can:
- Give the sound when shown any grapheme that has been taught
- Blend phonemes in order to read words
- Know most of the common grapheme-phoneme correspondences
- Read one-syllable and two-syllable words that can be de-coded phonically
- Apply phonic knowledge and skill as the prime approach to reading unfamiliar words that cannot be completely de-coded
- Read many frequently encountered words automatically
- Read three-syllable words that can be phonically de-coded
- Read a range of age-appropriate texts fluently
- Demonstrate understanding of age-appropriate texts

In Years 2, 3 and 4, meanwhile, inspectors are very likely to listen to two or three of the weakest readers reading their current book in order to evaluate the skills and knowledge that these weakest readers still need to learn as well as to assess the extent to which the book they are reading matches their current level of skill. Inspectors will also talk to students and ask them questions to determine the extent to which students can read. They are likely to focus their questions on students':
- Independence and choice
- Knowledge of books and individual authors
- Decoding strategies
- Comprehension including both literal and inferred meaning
- Support from home and school
- Enjoyment of reading
- Higher order reading skills such as identifying and understanding a book's style and themes, and similarities and differences between two or more books
- Awareness of own progress and development as a reader

Inspectors will investigate how successfully a school achieves its aim of ensuring that, by the end of Year 6, students have attained a Level 4 in reading by ensuring that students demonstrate an understanding of the ideas, themes, events and characters in a range of texts.

By the end of Year 9, students are expected to attain a Level 5, which requires them to understand a range of texts and select essential points, using inference and deduction, where appropriate. Inspectors will investigate how successfully a school has achieved this aim.

Inspectors are likely to ask the following questions of both primary and secondary schools:

1. Is attainment in English at any Key Stage below that found nationally?

2. Is attainment for English below the national floor standard?

3. Is attainment in English significantly lower than that in mathematics (or any other subjects at Key Stage 4 with proportionately large entries, e.g. science)

4. Is the attainment of any particular groups in English significantly lower than the average for the school and for all students nationally?

5. Is attainment in any of reading, writing or speaking and listening significantly lower than the other skills?

6. Is the attainment of any broad ability group in English significantly lower than others, especially those students who are working below expectations at the end of the previous key stage?

7. Is progress in English by the end of the key stage significantly below expectations?

8. Is progress in reading or writing significantly below expectations? Is there evidence that students leave the school without the expected level of reading skills?

9. Is progress in English for any particular group of students, including by prior attainment, significantly below expectations?

10. Does attainment and progress, overall and by groups, fluctuate over three years unrelated to any contextual factors in the students cohort?

It's wise to carry out your own investigations into each of the above areas and have ready answers - with evidence - for each of these questions.

It's also advisable to investigate the extent to which the teachers in your school:
- Develop students' reflective awareness of how to talk and work together
- Encourage students to express tentative ideas
- Model good talk skills in whole class discussions
- Scaffold group work but allow students to work independently of the teacher
- Plan group work which involves students 'thinking together'

Ultimately, though, there is only one measure of success in whole school literacy: Are more students at your school reading and writing better today as a result of your work? How can you demonstrate the impact of your actions on the reading and writing abilities of your students?

And that's HOW for now. Let's look at the WHAT...

CHAPTER FOUR

THE 'WHAT?'

We have considered the WHY and the HOW, now let's turn to the WHAT: what does literacy across the curriculum look like in practice? What tangible actions need to be taken in order to improve literacy learning?

I will divide the WHAT into three sections to reflect the three constituent parts of literacy:

1. Speaking and listening;

2. Reading; and

3. Writing.

The National Literacy Trust provide the following advocacy statement:

"Literacy skills are essential for young people to reach their potential in school and [to fulfil] opportunities throughout life. Every school needs a rigorous whole-school literacy policy which is implemented systematically across the curriculum and all teachers should view themselves as teachers of literacy, regardless of their subject specialism. Some schools have achieved this and as a result young people are able to not only access the curriculum, but have the tools to extend their thinking and knowledge with outstanding results."

At its most specific and practical, the term "literacy" applies to a set of skills that have long been accepted as fundamental to education. The Department for Education is clear and emphatic – the curriculum should offer opportunities for students to: "engage in specific activities that develop speaking and listening skills as well as activities that integrate speaking and listening with reading and writing". The curriculum should also offer opportunities for students to "develop speaking and listening skills through work that makes cross-curricular links with other subjects", to "develop reading skills through work that makes cross-curricular links with other subjects" and to "develop writing skills through work that makes cross-curricular links with other subjects".

The curriculum should also provide opportunities for students to "work in sustained and practical ways, with writers where possible, to learn about the art, craft and discipline of writing"; to "redraft their own work in the light of feedback [which could include] self-evaluation using success criteria, recording and reviewing performances, target-setting and formal and informal use of peer assessment"; to redraft in a purposeful way helping students to move "beyond proofreading for errors to the reshaping of whole texts or parts of texts".

It is common for any one of the strands – speaking and listening, reading, and writing – to be used as if it were synonymous with the wider concept of 'literacy'. However, when those in the wider world – employers, for example, or representatives of national or local government – complain about falling standards of literacy, they most often have in mind spelling, punctuation and grammar rather than the wider aspects of literacy outlined above.

'Literacy' is about more than SPaG...

The National Curriculum demands that connections are made between each of the three strands (speaking and listening, reading, and writing) and across subjects. This calls for students to develop their thought processes and understanding, as well as their abilities to recall, select and analyse ideas and information; and it calls for students to communicate in a coherent, considered and convincing way both in speech and in writing.

Accordingly, in order to develop their literacy skills, all students should be encouraged to:
- make extended, independent contributions that develop ideas in depth
- make purposeful presentations that allow them to speak with authority on significant subjects
- engage with texts that challenge preconceptions and develop understanding beyond the personal and immediate
- experiment with language and explore different ways of discovering and shaping their own meanings
- use writing as a means of reflecting on and exploring a range of views and perspectives on the world.

Let's now take a look at each of the three strands of literacy in turn starting with speaking and listening...

PART TWO

SPEAKING AND LISTENING

CHAPTER FIVE

AN INTRODUCTION TO
SPEAKING AND LISTENING

As Bob Hoskins huskily intoned, 'It's good to talk'.

The Russian psychologist, Lev Vygotsky, said that speaking and thinking were intricately linked because the process of speaking helps us to learn by articulating our thoughts and developing the concepts we use to understand the world. He argued that, "Up to a certain point in time, [thought and speech] follow different lines, independently of each other [but] at a certain point these lines meet, whereupon thought becomes verbal and speech rational".

Furthermore, Stricht's Law tells us that "Reading ability in children cannot exceed their listening ability" and Myhill and Fisher assert that "Spoken language forms a constraint, a ceiling not only on the ability to comprehend but also on the ability to write, beyond which literacy cannot progress".

Classroom talk, therefore, is an important part of literacy development because comprehension derives, not solely from writing and creating, but also from talking. Moreover, communication and understanding improve with practice. Therefore, providing students with an opportunity to talk in the classroom is vital if they are to develop their understanding.

Of course, talk in itself is not enough – classroom talk must be focussed on what needs to be developed. An unfocussed piece of writing will lead to unfocussed results, and so it is with speaking. There are a number of learning activities that help facilitate and support talk so that it is purposeful, structured, and appropriate which we'll come to in a moment...

Firstly, let's discuss the importance of exploratory talk in our classrooms. Exploratory talk is - as the name might suggest - talk which helps students to explore ideas in order to come to a better understanding of something. It is important that students are made to feel comfortable with one another and with their teacher so that they can begin to share incomplete ideas, revise their own thinking, and challenge each other's thinking.

Assessment for Learning guru Dylan William says that teachers in the UK are likely to ask more questions than teachers in the highest-performing countries and that we tend to think less about the questions we ask. In other words, we engage in Q&As whereby we ask a question - often closed - a student answers it, we respond then ask another question, ad infinitum. It's the same with how we group our students. The result being that we tend to fall into the familiar routine of asking our students to 'talk to your neighbour about...'.

The then much-maligned but now much-mourned National Strategies articulated a number of ways in which we can reinvigorate social groupings, building the groups around the intended purpose of the lesson. We'll take a look at some of those strategies in a moment but first let me defend group work...

Group work, it seems to me, is falling out of favour as a growing number of teachers reclaim direct instruction - chalk and talk - as the most effective strategy for teaching knowledge and skills. And there are some valid and convincing arguments against group work. For example, if it's not managed effectively it can lead to some students doing nothing - but when it is used wisely and managed well it can assist students' social development. Johnson and Johnson (1999) suggest that in order to create cooperative, purposeful group-work, five key ingredients are required:

1. Positive independence, so that students feel that their success is built upon needing to work together.

2. Face-to-face supportive interaction: they should actively help one another to learn and give each other positive feedback.

3. Accountability – individually and as a group – for their success.

4. Interpersonal skills: communication, trust, leadership, decision-making and conflict-resolution.

5. Group-processing: a level of reflection about how they have performed as a group and what they could do to improve.

Another advantage of group work for the teacher of literacy is that it can assist students' linguistic development. With this aim in mind, let's look at some group activities from the good old National Strategies which aim to promote classroom talk...

Circle Time can be used to share ideas, experiences, and feelings. Everyone sits in a circle and an item (such as a ball or cuddly toy) is held by whoever is speaking. The teacher sits in the circle and acts as a facilitator rather than a director. The rules for circle time should be discussed and agreed by all members. Three suggested rules are: 1. Only one person should speak at once - the talking object helps this rule, 2. You can "pass" if you don't want to speak about something, and 3. No put downs.

Pair Talk allows the articulation of ideas, encourages active listening and creates the right conditions for focused discussion. Using pairs also means that all students have more opportunity to speak and it assists those students who are less confident in larger groups. Use a stimulus, specific question or topic area for students to talk around. Model active listening and responding. Label as A and B to maintain on topic if not doing so (i.e. A is now listening and B talking then swap). Ask students to come up with questions they want answered individually which they then discuss in pairs. Set a target for pairs to achieve.

Think-Pair-Share is a structured way of developing ideas and thoughts. The teacher divides the class into groups of four. Each member of the group is assigned a letter A, B, C and D. The group is then divided into two pairs: A and B, and C and D. First, A interviews B whilst C interviews D. Then, the roles are reversed so that B interviews A whilst D interviews C. Finally, each student shares information about his/her partner in the group of four.

Listening Triads provide a structured means of eliciting information, developing concepts and understanding, and processing what is said. Students work in groups of threes adopting the roles of talker, questioner, recorder. The two students acting as talker and questioner sit facing each other, the recorder is slightly offset, observing rather than engaging. The talker starts by explaining something, by commenting on an issue, or by expressing an opinion. Next, the questioner prompts further explanation or seeks clarification on what the talker has said. The recorder makes notes throughout and gives a report at the end of the conversation. Next time, the roles are changed.

Envoys involve groups of three or four students and they promote active listening, public speaking and clarity of exposition, sharing and creating interdependence. Once each group in the classroom has carried out a task, one person from each group is selected as the 'envoy' and moves to a new group in order to explain and summarise what they've been discussing. The envoy then elicits information from the new group about what they'd thought, decided or achieved. The envoy then returns to their original group and feeds back. This is an effective way of avoiding tedious and repetitive 'reporting back' sessions in which the whole class has to listen to every group one by one.

Hot Seating is a dramatic device which encourages students to feel empathy with a character. It also encourages students to probe a character for information. It involves one student (or the teacher) sitting in the 'hot seat' at the front of the class or in the centre of a circle. The rest of the class acts as the audience facing the 'hot seat'. The student in the hot seat starts by expressing an opinion and then responds to questioning on the topic. The student can either express their own opinion or take a particular stance as dictated by the teacher. Alternatively, the student can assume the role of another person (real or imagined).

Freeze Frame, as the name suggests, involves groups of students creating a 'freeze frame' or a moment frozen in time which represents a feeling, a narrative, or a statement. A freeze frame is a point at which a film pauses. It is different to a still image because, with a freeze frame, there is action before and after the frozen moment but these are not seen by the audience. Once they have created their freeze frame, the groups show it to the rest of the class and they have to guess what it is and then discuss it.

Rotating Stations allows students to build on each others' ideas. The teacher assigns a series of 'stations' around the classroom, each 'station' has stimulus material plus paper and pens. The class is divided into groups and each group is located at a given station. Each group has ten minutes to discuss a topic and record their ideas on the paper provided. When their time is up, each group moves on to a new station - leaving the paper containing their notes behind - where they continue their discussion. Each new discussion is now influenced by the ideas the group encounters from the previous group to have stopped at that station. This rotation continues every ten minutes until each group has visited every station.

Rainbow Groups encourages students to listen (to their home group) and talk (to their colour group). First, a question is posed. Then, students have to provide an answer individually. Next, they share it with a partner and turn their two answers into one. The pair then join up with another pair and repeat the process. This way, four answers are synthesised into one.

Jigsaw, again involving groups of three or four students, is a structured way of dealing with a series of questions and of promoting team work. The advantage of a 'jigsaw' is that it offers a structure for group work, and promotes a range of speaking and listening. The teacher divides the whole class into small groups ensuring that each group reflects the balance of the whole class in terms of gender, ability, and attitude. Each group is given a common task, possibly set out on a worksheet (which is kept to a manageable length and complexity). If the groups are made up of four students then there are four questions within the main task – one for each member of the group. Questions are allocated to students in each group by the group through negotiation between students. All the students who have selected a particular question re-group into new 'expert' groups and work together on what is now a common problem. By the time this part of the lesson has been completed, each student has become an expert through discussion and collaboration with other 'experts'. Next, the original groups reform and the process of dissemination begins. The original groups are then set a final task which requires them to draw on the combined 'wisdom' of the group.

Philosophy for Students aims to encourage children to think critically, compassionately, creatively and collaboratively. This activity helps teachers to build a 'community of enquiry' where students pose a question then enquire into it. Students sit in a circle and use an object to indicate who is speaking. Stimulus material is placed around the room for students to view. The teacher introduces a topic and explains the process. Students are given a few minutes to move round the room and look at some of the stimulus material. When they return to the circle, they are given a couple of minutes to think of some questions related to the topic/stimulus that they would like to be answered. These questions are shared and a vote is taken on which question to discuss as a group. The teacher acts as the facilitator – reframing questions, adding supplementary questions, and mediating the group to ensure that everyone participates.

Value Continuum is a way for students to share their opinions, express their values, and engage in open discussion. The teacher identifies two locations at opposite ends of the classroom as representing two extremes of opinion. Students (or groups of students) then respond to statements made by the teacher by moving to a position between the two extremes which indicates to what extent they agree or disagree with the statement. If the activity involves groups rather than individual students, then the group must be afforded time to debate the statement and to reach agreement about their shared position.

Distancing uses narrative, drama, or role-play in order to distance students from sensitive, emotional or controversial subjects. For instance, instead of asking students to discuss their own feelings on, say, assisted suicide as part of a PSCHE lesson, the teacher may use a narrative from an old person who wishes to end their life at a time chosen by them and surrounded by family. The teacher then asks students to discuss how the person in the narrative may have felt.

Radio Phone-In involves the teacher or a student acting as a radio host with groups of three or four students playing the guests. The guests are given role-play cards which tells them what character to play. The rest of the class acts as the audience. The host discusses a topic with his/her guests. The guests respond to the topic according to their character. The audience then 'phones in' with questions. The questions act as a form of peer assessment and encourage enquiry.

TV Chat Show is similar to radio phone-in in that the teacher is the chat show host and students assume different characters discussing a topic. The audience asks questions, gets involved in the discussion, peer assesses and so on. The chat show could be a Parkinson-style affair or more like Jeremy Kyle.

CHAPTER SIX

THE THEORY OF
SPEAKING AND LISTENING

Let's take a detour to investigate the power of spoken language...

Catts et al, (2002) claim that our early years of development frame the rest of our lives and this is particularly true of literacy development because, without the spoken language skills needed to support the development of effective reading, academic success is limited. Low literacy skills are always being linked with poor attainment at school, and to physical and mental health, employment, socio-economic wellbeing, and involvement in the community in adult life.

There is no denying that our literacy skills have a significant impact on our personal, social and economic lives. At school, it should come as no surprise that spoken language has such a dramatic effect on attainment. After all, almost all classroom-based learning depends on spoken language.

It is impossible to understand written language without first acquiring a wide vocabulary as well as a familiarity with language structures. These are, according to Reese, Sparks & Leyva (2010) and Skeat et al, (2010), usually developed before a child begins school. Parents, therefore, are a child's first teacher. As parents interact with their children, they dig the foundations on which that child's language development will be built.

According to Morrow et al (1998), Fernald, Perfors & Marchman (2006) and Tomopoulos et al (2006), certain features of these early interactions are particularly important: for example, the frequency of one-to-one or small group interactions, the number and variety of words that children hear, and the reading aloud of story books. Fleer and Raban (2005) say that if children participate in rhyming games, singing and word play, their language skills will be enhanced further.

By engaging in such linguistic activity, young children grow to understand - albeit subconsciously - aspects of language that support their reading development. For example, when children make sounds and combine them into words and sentences, they begin to understand our phonological system including intonation and rhythm. This awareness of the separate sounds in words forms the basis for learning the written symbols that match those sounds. In other words, children begin to understand the alphabetic principle.

Spoken language builds children's vocabulary knowledge. Between the ages of two and six children's vocabulary explodes and this has a big influence on their later reading ability.

With this in mind, how can we as teachers help maximise our students' spoken language development?

We should plan to develop spoken language across all years and levels because it is not solely the domain of the early years teacher. All teachers should continue to help students become more articulate and sophisticated users of our language. Here are some practical ways of doing this:

1. Allow more wait time following a question. Typically, waiting at least 3 to 5 seconds for students to respond to a question is effective because it allows the "thinking time"

some young people need in order to process information before composing an answer. When wait time is increased, answers tend to be more complex.

2. Model the clear and correct use of spoken language. In other words, give unambiguous instructions, use accurate descriptive and positional language, utilise precise terminology where appropriate, and give clear feedback.

3. Regularly check for understanding until you have a clear idea of the level of your students' language skills. Sometimes, students who have trouble concentrating in class - particularly when the teacher is talking - may not actually understand what the teacher is saying. When you become aware of this, you can monitor your students' understanding and adjust your language when necessary. Of course, the student might just be naughty or you might just be boring!

4. Use simple, direct language and place verbs at the beginning of instructions. "Teacher talk" is not necessarily better than the language students access in other environments but it is different. As a result, students' language proficiency might be different from that required to access the curriculum, or even to understand simple classroom instructions. Confusion and disobedience can result from the fact that students are unfamiliar with the language structures and "lexical density" of the more formal teacherly language of the classroom. This does not mean that teachers should use the same language as students, but that they may need to use simpler language and emphasise important words.

5. Teach active listening skills. Some students can hear, but are not active listeners. Active listening requires selective and sustained attention, working memory, cognitive processing, and information storage and recall mechanisms. Teachers can help students develop these skills by giving them tasks such as listening for specific or key information, listening to answer specific questions, and listening to follow instructions.

6.	Teach note-taking skills whereby students have to write down the key points ascertained from a piece of spoken language.

7.	Build on students' language by elaborating on student's answers to questions, adding new information, extending the conversation through further questioning, or reinforcing the language through repetition.

8.	Develop communication skills such as turn-taking and the use of eye contact.

9.	Make sure the development of spoken language permeates the school day,. Spoken language is used all day, every day so take advantage and build spoken language activities into daily routines such as during tutor time (e.g. ask a question of each student that must be answered in a sentence), when handing out materials, when students enter and leave the classroom, and when giving instructions.

10.	Make sure students have the opportunity to speak. The teacher tends to dominate classroom discussion - and it is right that teachers do talk a lot because they have knowledge and experience to share. But it is also important that students get a chance to interact with the teacher and each other and to do so beyond responding to closed questions.

11.	Plan opportunities for one-to-one discussion. Spoken language develops best through paired conversation and when one of the people in the pair has a better developed vocabulary. Therefore, it is worth investigating ways of pairing up your students with people with more sophisticated language skills, perhaps an older student or a parent or volunteer. This could be a case of volunteers reading a book with a student or simply engaging in conversation. One to one conversation also enables young people to develop conversational skills such as turn-taking, intonation and eye contact.

12. Read lots of books together. Reading is the best way of developing a young person's vocabulary, particularly if you use the book as a stimulus. In other words, use the book as a means of initiating conversation by asking questions about the author's intentions, about the characters' motivations, and about the structure and plot, theme and genre, style and so on. Open questions such as 'What do you think is going to happen next and why?' are the most effective because they encourage students to develop their language and their cognition. For example, students have to make inferences and engage in critical thinking. Asking students to re-tell a story is also effective because it encourages them to master tense, sequencing, and logical reasoning, as well as expanding the imagination. You should never assume that students are too old to be read to: older students, including those in the sixth form, enjoy being told a story - as indeed do I! - and they can still learn from the experience because the teacher can highlight sophisticated vocabulary and syntactic structures which students may not pick up on if reading alone.

13. Think aloud. Model your cognitive processes, your logic and reasoning, by making visible the invisible act of thinking - in other words, make the implicit explicit. Self-talk is also useful in mediating situations - hearing how you process difficult situations helps students to use words to resolve an issue and encourages them to engage in their own self-talk, calming themselves down with language rather than with a physical act.

14. Plan opportunities to introduce any new vocabulary that is needed in the lesson. Think carefully when planning about the language demands of the lesson, particularly where a new vocabulary is required, and then explicitly teach this language. Whether it's the use of the passive voice in recipes in Food Technology or the use of comparative adjectives in Maths, you should think carefully about and then pay attention to the language demands of your lesson, making the implicit explicit.

15. Correct students' incorrect or inappropriate use of language. Explicitly teach the difference between formal and informal language, between standard English and regional dialects, and between technical and colloquial language and model how to use the appropriate tone, register and vocabulary. If students use language that is inappropriate in the context, correct them.

To conclude...

SOME SPEAKING AND LISTENING QUICK WINS:

1. Use fewer 'what?' questions and use more 'why?' and 'how?' questions
2. Give students time to rehearse answers to questions, perhaps by discussing their answers in pairs before sharing them more widely
3. Give students thinking time after each question has been asked before they are expected to share their answers
4. Enforce a 'no-hands-up' policy as often as possible
5. Model the kind of language you expect students to use in group discussions and answers
6. Build students' vocabularies by explicitly teaching the key words in your subject and by repeating key words as often as possible; give key words as homework, and test students on their spelling and meaning so that they become the expected discourse of all students

PART THREE

READING

CHAPTER SEVEN

AN INTRODUCTION TO READING

A useful starting point for teaching reading is to consider the reading skills we expect our students to use in our lessons. Asking teachers to consider what reading skills are required in their subjects is also an effective means of focusing teachers on the importance of literacy in those subjects.

Here are some possible questions to ask teachers:

1. Reading for information
- What kinds of text do you read in your subject?
- How do you read texts in your subject?
- What are the conventions of the texts you read in your subject?

2. Teaching vocabulary and spelling
- What are the most important words in your subject?
- Where can learners see these words and how do they learn their spelling and meaning?

3. Using layout to make handouts more accessible
- Are handouts clear and accessible?
- Are presentations uncluttered and in sensible colour combinations?
- Are key words listed at the beginning?
- Is the purpose of the text – why students are reading this/what they will learn – made explicit at the start?
- Are presentational features - such as columns, bullet points, captions, key words, etc. - used to make the text more accessible?

4. Promoting reading
- Do learners see you reading, and talking about reading?
- Does your classroom showcase some of the great writers from your subject and what they have written?
- Do you read texts aloud to the class?
- Do you talk about texts you are reading for pleasure?

Assessing reading comprehension

When assessing students' reading comprehension, common practice is to ask questions like 'Who said…?' and 'What happened when…?' But these types of question only test superficial reading skills. In order to test deeper reading skills, you need to use - and encourage all your colleagues to use - the following strategies:

Question variety
Use more open-ended questions such as 'Why?' and 'How?', and, rather than true/false questions, use question continuums whereby you ask students, on a scale of 1-5, how far do they agree.

Prediction
Ask students what they think happens next.

Cloze
Provide a text with key words missing and ask students to fill in the gaps.

Words to pictures
Ask students to draw a picture or graph to show what the text means.

Disjunction
Re-write the text but in the wrong order and ask students to organise it in the right order.

Making the implicit explicit

I've argued several times - and will continue to return to this refrain - that one of the secrets of effective literacy teaching is to make the implicit explicit, to make the invisible visible. In other words, you need to show your students what you do without thinking about it because you are an accomplished reader, writer and speaker of English. So what do experienced, effective readers like you actually do? What comes automatically once you're a mature and skilled user of language? You predict, skim, scan, question, empathise and infer. Let me explain…

Good readers make predictions or informed guesses about the text.

Good readers skim the text, reading quickly through sentences to get the 'gist'.

Good readers scan the text, quickly moving their eyes across a text searching for specific words.

Good readers ask questions about the text in order to clarify their thoughts.

Good readers move backwards and forwards through the text re-reading, making connections or clarifying ideas.

Good readers empathise   with the characters in the text, trying to understand how others think and feel.

Good readers visualise the text, creating images in their minds of what they are reading.

Good readers use inference, reading between the lines in order to uncover the writer's intended meaning.

CHAPTER EIGHT

READING ACTIVITIES

When I started teaching, DARTs were all the rage. Don't worry, I'm not about to wax lyrical about Eric Bristow's super-smashing-great arrows, I'm talking about Directed Activities Related to Texts. And like most of my wardrobe, it seems that DARTs are becoming fashionable once again.

DARTs require learners to interact with texts in a way that takes them beneath the surface. Here are some DARTs taken from the National Strategies:

Cloze - give students a text with some key words missing.

Why is this useful? Because students have to pay close attention to the meaning of the sentence, choose a word that fits grammatically, use their existing knowledge of the topic, work out what is likely from the rest of the text, what will fit with the style of the text, and whether a word has already occurred in the sentence, and pay close attention to the whole sentence by reading and rereading it.

Sequencing - give students a text that has been cut into chunks.

Why is this useful? Because students have to read and reread the text, pay close attention to the structure of the genre and to link words, locate the logic or guiding principle of the text, and use previous experience and prior reading.

Text marking - get students annotating or numbering a text to show sequence.

Why is this useful? Because students have to skim or scan the text to find specific information, differentiate between different categories of information, decide what is relevant information, find the main idea in a text, and question the information presented.

Text restructuring - get students to interpret a text in a different form, which might mean reading and then remodelling the information in another format such as a timeline, flowchart, list, map, chart, or rewriting in another genre.

Why is this useful? Because students have to identify what is key and relevant in a text, apply what they know in a new context, remodel the content and the format of the text, develop an awareness of the characteristics of different genres, summarise and prioritise information.

Over the next few pages I'm going to list some DARTs you could use with plays, poetry, and prose texts. They are offered in no particular order, simply as I've collated them over the years...

I

DARTS FOR PLAYS

Hot-seating character

Mock trials / inquiries

Debates

Shakespeare into soap

Play into prose

Act out a scene

Walking the Line: students walk around room speaking a line at a time, making sharp 90-degree turns at the end of each line.

Walking the Punctuation: students walk around room speaking the script but turning abruptly left or right at each punctuation mark.

Linked pairs:
- Mirror-mime: stand to face each other, one reads the script with actions; the other repeats language and movement.
- Back-to-back: students stand back to back, one reads the scripts; the other repeats.
- Changing style: one student reads script in a neutral tone; the other repeats back the language as a question, order, joke, sadly, fearfully etc.
- Forgetful actor: One student takes role of actor who can't remember his lines; the other is the prompter and holds the script.
- Puppet and puppeteer.

Reading script whilst performing an everyday action e.g. cleaning shoes, washing up, drinking at a bar etc.

Echoes: small groups – one student slowly speaks the lines, other echo every word to do with war/fighting etc.

Five investigations:
- Who are these characters? How can we portray them?What's going on? How can we portray it?
- Where does the scene take place? How can we show it?
- When does the action take place? How can we portray those times?
- Why do the characters behave as they do? How can we

portray those causes?

Student as director.

Banquo's ghost – one student as the ghost, the other as Macbeth. Ghosts pursue the fearful Macbeth who speaks various lines such as: Avaunt, and quite my sight!; Let the earth hide thee!; Thy bones are marrowless!; Thy blood is cold etc.

Finger-fencing with lines such as: Obey and go with me, for thou must die.

Choral speaking.

Shakespearean insults game.

Writing a newspaper e.g. Dunsinane Times inc. news items, advertisements, cartoons, crossword, readers' letters, sports page, travel page, jobs, gossip column, agony aunt, horoscopes, reviews, births, marriages and deaths etc.

Character's secret diaries.

Write a missing scene.

Storyboard a scene.

Sequencing.

Research into the playwright's life and times.

Other ideas specifically for use with Shakespeare plays:

Before introducing the play, get the class interested in the ideas or issues – e.g. talk about true love, love at first sight etc. as an introduction to Romeo and Juliet; talk about murder and ambition as an introduction to Macbeth; talk about sibling rivalry as an introduction to King Lear.

Get the class to act out a brief scene by reading the line to them and asking them to repeat it in character. Perhaps use a modern language version for this as a starting point to help them understand the plot – but retain some original language as a signpost for when they return to the text.

Ensure that all the class are involved by asking them to comment on what is happening in the play – or by playing the part of an Elizabethan audience and booing and hissing or cheering etc.

Don't give a plot overview before reading the text – or you are in danger of ruining their intrigue. Ask them what they think will happen next.

Divide a scene up and give different sections to different groups to rehearse. Then ask them all to act it out in sequence – perhaps with each group interpreting the text differently/with different emotions.

Have the whole class share the long soliloquies by reading to the next punctuation mark and swapping.

Get the class to sing lines to the tune of Christmas carols or popular nursery rhymes:

e.g. Sing the following prologue to Romeo and Juliet to Ba Ba Blacksheep, Jingle Bells or Rudolf the Red-Nosed Reindeer:

Two households, both alike in dignity,
In fair Verona, where we lay our scene,
From ancient grudge break to new mutiny
Where civil blood makes civil hands unclean.
From forth the fatal loins of these two foes
A pair of star-cross'd lovers take their life;
Whose misadventur'd piteous overthrows
Do with their death bury their parents' strife.

Or get the class to repeat each line with accompanying actions.

Get the class to act out short scenes.

Hot-seat characters from the play – e.g. have Lady Macbeth being interviewed. The class could ask her questions like:
- Do you believe your husband really met the witches on the heath?
- Do you love your husband?
- Would you contemplate killing your husband?
- Why did you not kill Duncan yourself?
- How has your baby's death affected you?

Get the class to transform the play into a tabloid news article – the first line of which must include the answers to the questions: Who? Why? Where? When?

Ask the class to summarise the play in less than 100 words.

Ask the class to choose 3 words of three columns of Shakespearian words to create an insult and stand them in two opposing lines. With each clap, one line will advance and shout their insult at the opposite line and vice versa.

II

DARTS FOR POETRY

Invent a new title

Write own poem based on title only

Write own final stanza

Convert prose into poetry, restoring line lengths etc.

Sequence jumbled stanzas

Group tableaux of moment in poem

Use favourite words to make a collage

Compare 2 poems

Storyboard / cartoon strip the poem

First Encounters:
- Listen to two readings of a poem and jot down instant reactions as a starter to a considered response.
- Listen to (in-house) taped readings
- Drip-feed the poem – read it once a week without comment
- Have a display board of (frequently changed and pupil-supplied) poems

Sharing and Presenting Poems:
- In groups, work out different ways of presenting poems dramatically to class
- Prepare own readings for performance and comparison
- Make taped readings – with sound effects – for other classes or exchange schools
- Choose slides to accompany a reading

Becoming Familiar with poems:
- Copy favourites into an accumulating personal anthology
- Make and display posters of poems
- Learn by heart

Exploring Poems:
- Group discussions, with guidance
- A and B write instant responses to poem, then exchange them and comment on each other's response
- Completion of poems with purposeful deletions
- Propose titles for untitled poems
- Sequence segments
- Spot the wrong word in a poem and propose a right one
- Parody
- Making or choosing pictures which capture the essence of a poem
- Invent the story behind the poem – what happened before, or happened off-page, or will happen next?
- Retell or reply to a poem from another point of view
- Rework in a different genre (e.g. newspaper) and discuss

what is gained or lost

Asking Questions:
- Groups prepare questions on a poem – for other groups or – as last resort- teacher
- Annotate the poem to answer questions expected of a foreign reader.

Collecting Poems:
- Prepare a thematic anthology
- Find poems in texts with other intentions – notices, newspapers, graffiti, tombstones
- Prepare 'With Great Pleasure', or 'Desert Island Poems' programmes

III

DARTS FOR PROSE

Predictions based on cover / title

Theme-based drama as introduction

Prose as script

Write a letter to one of the characters in the novel. Ask him/her questions as well as talking about yourself.

If you could change places with one of the characters, who would it be? Why ?

Which character is most like you? Why?

Create a newspaper page for one of the novels. Summarise the plot in one of your articles. Cover the weather in another. Include an editorial and a collection of ads that would be pertinent to the novel.

Summarise the plot by creating a cartoon version of the novel. Use about six to eight frames.

Rewrite a chapter or section of your novel from another character's point of view.

Why did the author write this particular story? Express your opinion.

Pretend you are a newspaper reporter whose job is to interview one of the characters. Write your interview.

You have become a character in one of the novels. Describe your experience during a conflict.

Write a poem about one of the novels. Touch on the characters, setting, plot, and theme.

Rewrite a portion of the novel as a play.

Redesign the front and back cover of your novel. Include the pertinent information as well as a blurb on the back.

Pretend you are a character in the book and write a diary.

Write and perform a play based on the story.

Make a timeline of the events of the story. Explain it.

Write and perform a TV commercial to sell the book.

Make a comic book based on the book.

Research and prepare a report on the author's life. Present it to the class.

Write and record a radio advertisement that will make people want to read the story.

Create a poster advertising the book. Explain it.

Write and illustrate a poem about the story.

Design the front page of a newspaper with headlines and a story about what happened in the book.

Draw a film poster advertising the story, and cast a real actor in each character's role. Explain your choice of casting.

Write and illustrate a children's book summarising the story for someone younger.

Write a letter to a character explaining your reaction to him or her in the book.

Write a letter to the author giving your reactions to the book.

Write a book review that might be published in the newspaper.

Write an agony aunt column for all of the characters in your story. Respond to their problems.

Choose one character in this story. Think about what the character was like at the beginning of the story. Write about how the character has changed by the end of the story. What events led up to the changes of the character?

Pretend that you have been chosen to write a sequel to this story. Write a brief summary of the sequel. Include information about the sequel's plot, setting and main characters.

Summarise the plot of your story by creating a cartoon version of the story. Use about 6 to 8 frames.

Make a travel poster inviting tourists to visit the setting in your book.

Write a poem about your story. Include characters, setting, plot, and theme.

IV

A HIERARCHY OF READING COMPREHENSION

We'll end this chapter by looking at some useful questions to ask students when you're reading a text in class. These questions reflect a hierarchy of comprehension skills. As we get better at reading we move from 'what' (a basic level of comprehension) to 'who' (being able to comment on who wrote a text and who it is aimed at) to the higher level skills, which involve analysis and evaluation: the 'how' of a text.

What:
- What is the text about?
- What type of text is it (informative, descriptive, entertaining, persuasive, etc.)?

Who:
- Who wrote it?
- Who is it written for (a general/specific audience, male/female, young/old, etc.)?

How is divided into three:
1. Structure
2. Sentences (or syntax)
3. Words

Structure:
- Chronological (a story told in sequence from the beginning to the end) or non-chronological (a newspaper article starting with the key facts)? Why?
- Short/long paragraphs? Note form? Bullet-points? Why?
- How are ideas linked together (logically using connectives such as 'firstly' and 'secondly' or 'therefore' and 'however')?

Sentences:
- Questions, commands, exclamations, statements? Why?
- Short or long? Why?
- Formal or colloquial? Why?

Words:
- Formal '(do not' and 'cannot') or informal ('don't' and 'can't')?
- Personal ('I'/'you') or impersonal ('it')? Active ('you pour the liquid') or passive ('pour the liquid')?
- Serious or funny?
- General ('clear') or specialist ('diaphanous')?
- Easy ('lazy') or difficult ('languorous')?

CHAPTER NINE

THE THEORY OF READING

In this chapter we are going to take a look at some of the theory behind the art of reading…

Reading can helpfully be broken down into the following constituent parts:
- Phonics
- Vocabulary
- Fluency
- Comprehension

Phonics is about recognising and understanding individual sounds and the letters that represent them. Vocabulary is about the number and variety of words we can understand and about understanding words in their different contexts. Fluency is about reading a text quickly and accurately, adopting the appropriate intonation. Comprehension is about engaging with a text at a deep level by understanding word meanings, and the syntactic and semantic relationships between words.

We'll take a look at each of these parts in turn and then, in the next chapter, explore the practice of guided reading as a means of helping our students to develop their phonemic awareness, vocabulary, fluency and comprehension, as well as other strategies for developing our students' comprehension skills.

So, without further ado, let's get started with phonics…

I

PHONICS

Phonics is often confused with phonemic awareness but, although phonics depends on phonemic awareness, the two terms are not synonymous. So let's start with some definitions…

Phonological awareness is a broad term referring to the ability to focus on the sounds of speech as distinct from its meaning: on its intonation or rhythm, on the fact that certain words rhyme, and on the separate sounds. When children play with language by repeating syllables, they are demonstrating an awareness of the phonological element of rhyme.

Phonemic awareness, meanwhile, is a subset of phonological awareness and is the most important phonological element in the development of reading and spelling. Phonemic awareness is the ability to focus on the separate, individual sounds in words which are called the 'phonemes'. Phonemes are the smallest unit of sound that make a difference to a word's meaning. Thus if you change the first phoneme in the word man from /m/ to /t/, you change the word from man to tan.

Phonemic awareness is a prerequisite for learning an alphabetic code: if children cannot hear the separate sounds in words (and certain English sounds do not exist in some other languages), they cannot relate these sounds to the letters of the alphabet and so cannot use decoding skills to analyse unknown words.

Phonics refers to the relationship between individual sounds (phonemes) and the letters that represent them (graphemes). A phoneme is often represented by a single letter, but can be represented by two letters (e.g. -ck in the words *tick*), by three letters (e.g. -igh in the word *high*) and even by four letters (e.g. -ough in the word *although*). Phonics is also the term used to describe the teaching of letter-sound relationships.

There exists a broad hierarchy of phonological skills as follows:
- Rhythm and rhyme
- Onset and rime
- Phonemic awareness
- Isolation
- Blending
- Segmentation
- Manipulation

Rhythm and rhyme

Rhyming is a particularly important component of early language experiences. Children who cannot recognise or generate rhyme are at risk of not developing the skills they need to be successful in using familiar word parts for reading and spelling.

Children usually become aware of rhythm first as they develop their understanding of the English language. Syllables provide the rhythm and children are often introduced to rhythm by clapping the beats in their name or in other polysyllabic words. Chunking words into syllables is an important strategy for developing both reading and spelling skills. Once children have become aware of rhythm, they usually become aware of rhyme - that certain words sound the same at the end.

How can teachers help children to develop an awareness of rhythm and rhyme? Understanding the concept of rhyme requires a student to know which part of the word is important for rhyming so teachers need to model their recognition and production of rhyme.

If children can recognise and produce rhyming patterns - such as cop, hop, mop, top - they are actually demonstrating early phonemic awareness because they are deleting the first phoneme (the onset) in the syllable and replacing it with another. While they are initially unaware they are doing this, the process enables students to learn that words are made up of a sequence of single sounds. It's important, therefore, that teachers include word play and rhyming activities in their teaching.

These two early levels of phonological awareness – rhythm and rhyme – usually take place in the Early Years stage and lead onto the development of more advanced phonological skills which are required for the development of reading.

Onset and rime

Onset and rime are divisions within a syllable. The onset is made up of the parts of the syllable that come before the vowel; the rime is the vowel and all subsequent consonants. All syllables have a rime, but not all have an onset. The word 'at', for example, has no letters before the vowel, therefore has no onset. The word 'mat', on the other hand, has the onset 'm' and the rime 'at'. The word 'strike' has the onset 'str' and the rime 'ike'. According to Gunning (2001), children naturally use the onset-rime division in their early attempts at segmenting syllables. While many children do not need practice of this intermediate step before phonemic awareness, it can be important for some.

Activities which involve verbal rhyming develop students' understanding of onset and rime. Creating words that have a common rime, perhaps using letter cards, is also effective.

Phonemic awareness

Phonemic awareness is the ability to recognise single sounds, as well as to play with them, blend them together, segment them, and move them around. Phonemic awareness is crucial for reading because phonemes are the building blocks of reading and writing.

Children need to be able to identify separate sounds in a word - or phonemes - before they can link letters to sounds, which is important in an alphabetic language like English.

Understanding the different levels of phonemic skill development and how to teach each level, using examples in a logical sequence, is important - particularly for those students who have difficulty acquiring these skills.

Phoneme isolation

Phoneme isolation is the ability to recognise the separate phonemes in words, literally isolating each sound. The first phoneme in a syllable is the easiest to identify, then the final phoneme, then the middle one.

When children have difficulty with this, the teacher should explicitly model the process, identifying the separate phonemes in a series of words.

Phoneme blending

Phoneme blending involves listening to a sequence of phonemes read aloud and then combining them all into a word.

Once children have mastered this, so-called 'stop' consonants should be introduced. Stop consonants are those which cannot be continued with distorting them, such as 'p', 'b', 'g', 'd' and 't'.

Teachers needs to make sure they do not distort the phonemes when teaching children stop consonants. For example, the word 'cat' should be said "caaat" not "caaatuh". It's equally important that the initial consonant is not distorted, e.g. "caaat"not "cuh-aaat".

Phoneme segmentation

Phoneme segmentation involves counting or tapping out each sound in a word as they are spoken. The teacher needs to model this process aloud before giving students plenty of opportunities to copy the model and try out examples of their own. For example, in 'at' there are two phonemes to count or tap; in 'cat' there are three; and in 'cart' there are four and so on.

Phoneme manipulation is the ability to manipulate sounds in order to form different words. This process helps develop students' sound knowledge as a component of the reading and writing. Deleting, adding, and combining phonemes are a part of this manipulation. Again, the teacher should begin by modelling this process before encouraging students to try it for themselves. For example: hear the word 'Spain' without the 's' = pain; what word would we get if we added 's' to the beginning of 'mart' = smart; what word would we get if we took the 's' away from 'strap' = trap; and what word would we get if we took the 's' away from 'strap' and put it at the end = traps.

Much of what we've discussed in this section on phonics has been for teachers in Early Years but it is useful for all teachers of literacy - and, yes, that means you - to be aware of these skills because children develop language at different stages. An awareness of phonics instruction is also useful for teachers when they are introducing new vocabulary such as technical subject-specific words which are unfamiliar to students.

On average, though, this is the usual sequence for teaching phonics:

1. Teach students to discriminate separate phonemes (phoneme isolation)

2. Teach students letter-sound relationships (phonemic and phonic skills)

3. Introduce new letters by the sound they represent not by the letter

4. Teach sounds along with the letters of the alphabet to help students see how phonemic awareness relates to reading and writing

5. Teach students how to manipulate sounds through blending and segmenting which helps them read words

6.   Teach students how to segment sounds with letters to help them spell words

7.   Where necessary, teach students the letter names and shapes

Research (e.g. Armbruster, Lehr & Osborn, 2003) suggests that for most children the above process should take no more than around 20 hours which might be achieved by dedicating between 10 and 15 minutes a day during the first two terms of Reception. After this period, phonics instruction should continue in order to consolidate the development of students' phonemic skills.

Of course, some students will take considerably longer than others and this process may still be developing after two or more years of schooling. Research suggests that there is little to be gained by persisting with phonemic skills only at the spoken level without reference to letters after the first year of school. Instead, the two (sounds and letters; spoken and written) are best taught together.

Here are some general tips for teaching phonics:

1.   Ensure that everyone working with students in their phonemic awareness groups (teachers, support staff, volunteers) can articulate the sounds being taught accurately and clearly.

2.   When letters are first introduced, they should be referred to by the sound they represent, not by the letter name. It is the sound that will help students with the blending process.

3.   Work in small groups of four to six students for phonemic awareness training for all students if possible.

4.   Work in groups of between one and three with students who are having difficulties.

5.   Concentrate on blending and segmenting, the most

important phonemic skills for reading and spelling.

6. Build from easy to hard when constructing practice items for students

7. Give students multiple opportunities to practise. They should complete at least three successful practice items at least three days in a row before you can be confident they have achieved the skill. You should then review the skill a week or two later.

Phonics instruction is not a complete reading curriculum and cannot guarantee reading and writing success for all students. It will, however, provide the foundation upon which independent reading, writing and spelling can be built. The overall success of a reading curriculum will depend on the effectiveness of the entire literacy curriculum, and the extent to which it provides different levels of support for the wide range of student needs present in most classrooms.

II

VOCABULARY

Vocabulary is critical to success in reading as well as academic achievement more generally. The size of a student's vocabulary in their early years of schooling (the number and variety of words that the young person knows) is a significant predictor of reading comprehension in later schooling and in life. Most children are experienced speakers of the language when they begin school but reading the language requires more complex, abstract vocabulary than that used in everyday conversation. Children who have had stories read to them during the first years of their lives are exposed to a much broader and richer vocabulary than those contained in everyday conversations and, as such, arrive at school better prepared for reading. For this reason, teachers need to understand the importance of the role of vocabulary and directly support its development so that children who are not exposed to reading before they start school are helped to catch up.

Learning vocabulary is an incremental process. Our understanding of a word grows with repeated exposure to it. Dale & O'Rourke (1986) say that learning vocabulary takes place on a continuum, ranging from never having seen or heard a word before to having a deep knowledge of that word and its different meanings, as well as the ability to use that word confidently and accurately in both speaking and writing. Acquiring vocabulary is incremental because words differ in many ways: they differ according to syntax – knowing what part of speech a particular word is can assist reading; they differ according to the size of their 'family' – knowing one of a family of words will help the reader determine a number of others; some words are *polysemous* which means they can have multiple meanings (e.g. the word 'scale' means to climb, a feature of a fish, a plant disease, a measuring instrument, the ratio of distance on a map to that on the ground, and much more. Students who know multiple meanings of words are more prepared to read widely and across multiple contexts.

In short, vocabulary is complex but also vital to developing reading comprehension. Let's look at why this is…

If a student knows the meaning of the word *happy*, and knows the single letter-sounds that make that word, then the word can be easily decoded and understood when read in a text. The words *happier* and *happiness* are also more likely to be read and understood. With only a few exposures, these words will be familiar enough to be recognised on sight and so a student's reading vocabulary grows.

Young people who develop reading skills early in their lives by reading regularly add to their vocabularies exponentially over time. This is sometimes called 'The Matthew Effect' after the line in the Bible (Matthew 13:12), "The rich shall get richer and the poor shall get poorer". In the context of literacy, the Matthew Effect is that 'the word rich get richer while the word poor get poorer'. Daniel Rigney explains: "While good readers gain new skills very rapidly, and quickly move from learning to read to reading to learn, poor readers become increasingly frustrated with the act of reading, and try to avoid reading where possible.

Students who begin with high verbal aptitudes find themselves in verbally enriched social environments and have a double advantage. Good readers may choose friends who also read avidly while poor readers seek friends with whom they share other enjoyments." (*The Matthew Effect*, Daniel Rigney).

Furthermore, E D Hirsch, in his book *The Schools We Need*, says that "The children who possess intellectual capital when they first arrive at school have the mental scaffolding and Velcro to catch hold of what is going on, and they can turn the new knowledge into still more Velcro to gain still more knowledge".

Department for Education research suggests that, by the age of seven, the gap in the vocabulary known by children in the top and bottom quartiles is something like 4,000 words (children in the top quartile know around 7,000 words). The word poor can not catch up with the word rich because to do so they'd need to be able to learn more words more quickly than the word rich.

A student who does not know the meaning of the word *happy* will struggle over that and related words (e.g. happiness, happier, happiest, unhappy) in connected text, even if he can decode them, because transforming letters into words is useless if those words do not have a meaning.

If a student continues to experience frustration when reading because he is word poor, then he is likely to give up, denying himself of the opportunity to build vocabulary, fluency and world knowledge.

Young people who do not acquire these skills easily will become increasingly disadvantaged over time. Vocabulary helps to build comprehension and is therefore a key tool for reading comprehension. Young people who lack vocabulary and prior knowledge (context) will have difficulty understanding the books they encounter in school, especially as those books become more difficult.

So what can we do to help the word poor become richer?

One answer is to plan group work activities which provide an opportunity for the word poor to mingle with the word rich, to hear language being used by students of their own age and in ways that they might not otherwise encounter.

Another answer is to model higher-order reading skills because, as the literate adults in the room, we teachers use these skills unconsciously all the time so we need to make the implicit explicit. For example, we could model:
- Moving quickly through and across texts
- Locating key pieces of information.
- Following the gist of articles
- Questioning a writer's facts or interpretation
- Linking one text with another
- Making judgments about whether one text is better than, more reliable than, or more interesting than another text

We can promote the love of reading for the sake of reading, too; encouraging our students to see reading as something other than a functional activity. It is the responsibility of every adult working in a school (not just teachers, and certainly not just English teachers) to show that reading because we like reading is one of the hallmarks of civilised adult life.

But perhaps the most effective way of helping the word poor to become richer is to explicitly teach vocabulary. This may sound old fashioned but often the old ways are the best ways. Let's take a closer look at the role of direct instruction…

There is a growing weight of evidence (for example, Beck & McKeown, 2007, Rinaldi, Sells & McLaughlin, 1997, and Beck, McKeown & Kucan, 2008) suggesting that direct instruction works, because it can add substantially to the vocabulary growth of all students.

According to Allen (1999), direct instruction also helps students to become more proficient as readers and thinkers in both fiction and non-fiction, develops a "deeper understanding of the words and concepts students are partially aware of, nurtures understanding of new concepts, increases reading comprehension and enhances both oral and written communication skills".

Beck and McKeown (2007) argue that the best way of teaching vocabulary is to select 'quality' words that regularly appear in texts appropriate to the student's age but which can also be useful in different contexts, and then to teach those words in depth.

Biemiller (2010), meanwhile, argues that the best way of teaching vocabulary is to teach as many new words as possible, albeit in less depth, in order to increase a student's chances of growing their vocabulary.

Pressley et al (2007) advocate teaching a range of long-term vocabulary.

Each approach has been shown to have some impact.

Let's now take a look at some practical strategies - which go beyond the use of key words - to build vocabulary instruction into everyday routines…

In order to make vocabulary instruction a part of everyday classroom routine, you might model high quality language, reading aloud to students from high quality literature. We've already seen that written vocabulary is more extensive and varied than spoken vocabulary so reading a book several times to younger students can provide the kind of repeated exposure to new vocabulary that is necessary for word knowledge to become more secure. You can supplement this by making audio books available for students to use independently and by actively modelling good language.

You might also give thought to the language you use when giving instructions - using increasingly sophisticated vocabulary along with definitions where necessary.

You might utilise the involvement of parents and other volunteers (including older students such as sixth formers) to regularly meet with students to talk about books or a topic being studied in class.

You might discuss key words before reading the text in which they appear because when we have previous experience of something, we can encode new information about it more effectively and more richly. Let's take a short detour into schema theory at this point...

According to Harvey & Goudvis (2000), schema theory is the notion that our previous experiences, knowledge, and emotions affect what and how we acquire new information. In the case of reading comprehension, *schema* is the kind of background knowledge and experience we bring to a new text. The word rich draw on prior knowledge and experience to help them understand what they are reading and then they use that knowledge to help them make new connections. The word poor, however, often read through a text without stopping to consider whether or not the text makes any sense to them based on their own background knowledge and do not consider whether or not their knowledge can be used to help them understand confusing or challenging ideas and words.

It follows therefore that teaching students how to connect a new text to their prior knowledge will help them to better comprehend what they're reading. Keene and Zimmerman (1997) say that we should teach students to make three types of connections: how to connect a new text - though this theory could be applied to any form of information - to they own experiences (text to self), to other texts they've read (text to text), and to the wider world (text to world).

To make vocabulary teaching a part of everyday classroom practice, you might also decide which words to teach by drawing on great works of fiction and non-fiction. In deciding which words to focus on, you might ask yourself the following questions: Which words are most important to understanding the situation or the text? Which words will help build important concept knowledge? Which words will be encountered frequently outside this particular context? Which words have multiple meanings? Which words can be figured out from the context?

Beck (2002) devised a three-tier system to help teachers decide which words to teach. It went like this:

Tier 1 words: basic and high frequency words which are used in everyday conversation, such as *mother*, *said* and *house*. Most children will learn these words relatively quickly through frequent exposure. There is no need to explicitly teach these words through direct instruction.

Tier 2 words: words which appear more frequently in written language than in spoken language, and used by language users of different ages. Tier 2 words can be used across contexts to add clarity and/or descriptive power.

Tier 3 words: word which relate to specific fields of knowledge, such as the sciences. For example, *mesa*, *xylem* and *annulus*. These words should be explicitly taught as part of subject-specific literacy as and when required.

Beck recommends focusing on Tier 2 words for direct instruction because these are the words that will be most useful across a range of contexts and yet are words that students are less likely to learn independently.

Beck also shares a sequence for teaching word meanings. The focus word is normally a word that students have encountered in a text being read in class. Once the word has been brought to the class's attention, the teacher should:

1.   Read the sentence in which the word appears aloud to the class

2.   Show students the word written down and ask them to say it aloud

3.   Ask students to repeat the word several times

4.   Brainstorm possible meanings with the class

5. Point out any parts of the word which might help with meaning, for example a prefix or Greek or Latin root

6. Reread the sentence to see if there are any contextual clues

7. Explicitly explain the meaning of the word through simple definition and the use of synonyms

8. Provide several examples of the word being used in context, emphasising the word

9. Ask questions to determine whether or not students have understood the word

10. Provide some sentences for students to judge whether or not the word is used correctly

11. Get students to write their own sentences using the word

12. Explicitly use the word during the course of the next few days in order to reinforce its meaning.

One of the advantages of this sequence is that it ensures students are exposed to new vocabulary several times and get to see, hear and use new words in context.

Another useful strategy is to use graphic organisers in order to explain the meaning of words. For example, graphic organisers - such as concept maps, word trees, and word maps - can be used to show the relationships between words.

III

FLUENCY

Fluency is the ability to read text quickly and accurately, adopting the appropriate intonation. Fluency requires a background knowledge of the text, as well as a rapid retrieval of the requisite vocabulary. Fluency also requires a knowledge of syntax and grammar in order to predict the words that are likely to appear next.

The other day, my Kindle e-reader provided me with a perfect example of what fluency means. I was stuck in a traffic jam and had long grown tired of the radio so plugged my Kindle into the MP3 socket of my car. I switched the book I was reading to 'text to speech' mode which means the words are read aloud by an automated voice. The narrator sounds a bit like Stephen Hawking having a stroke but the technology serves a purpose. However, because the voice is automated, it doesn't read with fluency. The words do not always (ever) have the appropriate intonation and the narrator does not take account of context. For example, in one sentence the narrator pronounced "read" as the present tense 'reed' rather than the past tense 'red' as it should have been. Hearing such heinous crimes against grammar, I naturally winced. It was like listening to one of Year 7 students stumbling over a Spenserian sonnet with all the grace and decorum of a drunk tramp at a funeral.

The ability to adapt one's vocabulary and intonation according to a text's syntax and grammar, and the ability to read ahead assists with both speed and accuracy. Experienced readers integrate these processes so that reading becomes automatic - done without thinking - which allows their cognitive energy to be focused on the task of discerning meaning. A useful analogy is learning to tie your shoe laces. When you first learn to tie your laces, because it is unfamiliar, you have to dedicate all your attention to it. You concentrate on tying the laces and so cannot engage in conversation. However, once you have mastered the art of lace-tying - through repeated exposure to it - you begin to do it automatically, without having to think about it. Now, you perform the task out of habit without using any cognitive energy and that allows you to talk whilst tying your laces.

There is a strong correlation between fluency and reading comprehension; indeed, it is such a strong link that fluency and comprehension can be regarded as interdependent. After all, fluency only occurs when a reader understands the text; if reading is hesitant and disjointed, meaning is lost.

What is fluency?

It is impossible to be a fluent reader if you have to keep stopping to work out what a word is. To be fluent you have to move beyond the decoding stage to accurately read whole words. Therefore, one of the first skills to teach in order to achieve fluency is *accuracy*.

A fluent reader has ready access to a vast bank of words which can be used in different contexts. The words to which a reader has immediate access are called their 'sight vocabulary'. Even complex words that originally had to be decoded – like 'originally' and 'decoded' rather than monosyllabic function words like 'that' and 'had' – but which can now be recognised on sight, become a part of the fluent reader's lexicon. But recognition is not enough for fluency: as well as being in the reader's sight vocabulary, words must also be stored in their 'receptive vocabulary' - that is to say, words which the reader knows the meaning of. The larger the bank of words that are both recognised and understood on sight, then the broader the range of texts which are accessible. For this reason, developing students' sight vocabularies and receptive vocabularies are the most effective ways of developing both fluency and reading comprehension.

Once your students' sight and receptive vocabularies have been developed, you must make sure that the texts to which you expose students are appropriate to their age and reading ability so that they do not contain unfamiliar or technical words that are outside students' knowledge base. This is why early readers need simple texts to help them develop both speed and confidence. Although it's sometimes tempting to give students 'harder books' - as a way of challenging them - this is not always the best approach. Texts within a students' knowledge base provide them with opportunities to practise their vocabulary, develop appropriate expression, and build confidence and belief in themselves as readers.

Once you've developed accuracy, you need to develop *speed*, increasing the rate at which your students can access texts.

Reading speed is also strongly linked with reading comprehension. When a reader is both accurate and quick, word identification becomes automated and they no longer require cognitive energy or attention, thus freeing up precious space in the working memory for higher order comprehension.

Reading speed is not the same as reading fast. People who read too quickly and therefore show no regard for punctuation, intonation or comprehension are not fluent readers. Reading speed is about being able to process texts quickly whilst understanding the text and taking account of punctuation and adopting an appropriate intonation. In short, improving students' reading speed is important but it must not be at the expense of comprehension.

As a 'back of an envelope' calculation, the average reading speed in the primary phase is as follows:
- by end Year 1 = 60 words per minute
- by end Year 2 = 90/100 words per minute
- in years 3 to 6 = 100–120 words per minute with fewer than 3 errors

After accuracy and speed, _prosody_ - that is to say, reading with expression - is the third component of reading fluently. Prosody is more difficult to achieve than accuracy and speed because it involves developing stress, pitch, and rhythm. However, Prosody is essential in rendering reading aloud meaningful.

Poor prosody can cause confusion and has an impact on readers' interest and motivation to read. Good prosody, meanwhile, makes reading aloud come alive and reflects the author's message more accurately and more meaningfully.

So how do we help students to develop fluency?

1. One of the best ways for teachers to help students develop fluency is to read aloud to them in an engaging and motivating way in order to model fluency for them. Doing all the voices, adding sound effects and dramatic pauses, heightens students' engagement.

2. Using 'fluency cards' which contain lines of single letters and common letter combinations can also help students to develop fluency because fluency is achieved through automatic recognition of words and parts of words including letter sounds.

3. Another way of increasing students' fluency is to display high frequency irregular words. Word walls - when they are referred to and used in competitions or quizzes - help build students' automatic recognition of words.

4. Students may also need direct instruction in how to read punctuation. Most students, although they know how to punctuate their writing, have no idea how to read punctuation.

5. Whole class reading of short pieces of dialogue is a low risk activity - particularly when the teacher reads the passage first then students repeat it - to build fluency in lower ability readers.

6. Repeatedly reading a text provides the practice needed to develop accuracy, speed and confidence. A typical strategy is to pair students up and for the more fluent reader in the pair to model the appropriate rate and intonation for the less fluent reader who then repeats the passage. Alternatively, both students could read simultaneously. The more fluent reader in the pair is likely to start fractionally ahead of the less fluent reader, modelling accuracy, rate and intonation, but as the less fluent reader gains in confidence, the two students will blend together.

7. Reading lots of poetry - as well as being enjoyable in itself - helps develop reading fluency because poetry tends to have a natural rhythm when it is read aloud.

8. Get students reading aloud from a script, say a monologue or short scene. The focus is not on dramatic kinaesthetic performance but on interpreting the text using only the voice. Students are encouraged to bring the plot to life

9. Listen to audio books or ask older volunteers (parents, local people, sixth formers) to record their favourite stories to play to

the class.

COMPREHENSION

Understanding what a text means is about much more than decoding or word recognition. The depth of understanding differentiates the weak reader from the strong reader.

Comprehension is an active process which is heavily dependent on the reader's spoken language skills, as well as their understanding of word meanings and the syntactic and semantic relationships between words. Comprehension is the ability to engage with a text at a deep level.

Paris & Myers, (1981), Pressley, (1998), and Torgesen, (1982; 2000) share four behaviours which are associated with good reading comprehension:

1. Good readers are purposeful: good readers understand the purpose of their reading, and so are able to adjust their reading style accordingly. In other words, they know *why* they are reading and *how* they should read. They can skim the contents page, chapter headings, and paragraph openings to get the gist of a text and to extract key information which enables them to interpret what a text means on the basis of their prior knowledge.

2. Good readers understand the purpose of the text: good readers are not only purposeful themselves, but they also understand that writers are purposeful. A writer may wish to provide very simple information (e.g. instructions for assembling a cabinet) or more complex information (e.g. a report on stem cell research). A writer may wish to persuade, inform or entertain the reader. A writer may wish to present opinions as indisputable fact. Understanding a writer's purpose makes good readers aware of how particular literary devices are being used to influence their response.

3. Good readers review their comprehension: good readers constantly review, analyse and asses their comprehension in order to ensure there are no gaps in their understanding. They relate information in a text to their own experiences or prior knowledge, and evaluate information in order to determine whether it confirms or contradicts what they already know. Good readers ask questions as they read and search for the answers in the text.

4. Good readers adjust their reading strategies: good readers are able to adjust their reading strategies, slowing their reading speed when sentences are long and complex, re-reading a section if they begin to lose meaning, and drawing inferences from surrounding text or using their letter-sound knowledge in order to help construct the meaning of unfamiliar words. Good readers can also pause to take notes which help them retain complex information.

These four behaviours are typical of active readers, people who engage with a text, as opposed to passive readers who do not.

Active engagement with a text depends not only on the skill of the reader, but also on the nature of the text. Broadly speaking, texts can be divided into three levels of comprehension: independent level; instructional level; and frustration level. It's important to know which kind of text to give to students in different situations. To explain why, let's take a short diversion into the zone of proximal development…

The Russain psychologist Lev Vygotsky had a theory that teachers should only give students work to do which falls within 'the zone of proximal development'. He defined this zone as "the distance between the actual developmental level as determined by independent problem-solving and the level of potential development as determined through problem-solving under adult guidance, or in collaboration with more capable peers". (Vygotsky, 1978) In other words, teachers should not give students work to do which they have already mastered, nor work which they cannot possibly master yet. Instead, teachers should give students work to do which they can master if they think hard about it and if they have help.

If the work is too easy, students will do it automatically and learn nothing. If the work is too hard, however, students won't be able to do it and will become demotivated. But if the work is just hard enough that students are challenged by it but can achieve it, they will extend their learning.

Daniel Willingham, the cognitive scientist, echoed Vygotsky when he said that "working on problems that are of the right level of difficulty is rewarding, but working on problems that are too easy or too difficult is unpleasant". The pleasure is in the solving of the problem. Working on a problem with no sense that you're making progress, by contrast, is not pleasurable; it is frustrating.

I like to think of this in terms of Goldilocks and the Three Bears. Heartless criminal Goldilocks - having illegally entered someone else's property, proceeded to pilfer her way from room to room. In the kitchen, she tried three bowls of porridge: one belonged to Baby Bear but that was too cold; one belonged to Daddy Bear but that was too hot; one belonged to Mummy Bear and that was just right. ('Cooking just doesn't get tougher than this,' she muttered to herself as she wiped her fingerprints from the spoon and made off with her loot.)

Texts can be viewed in the same way as the porridge Goldilocks nicked... some texts are too easy, some texts are too hard; but other texts are just right.

Let's take a closer look at the three levels of text difficulty...

Independent level AKA cold porridge

At this level, the reader is able to read most or all of the text with fluency, finding no more than about one word out of every twenty challenging. Students should be given texts which are at their independent level for independent reading activities. By reading fluently, students will be able to engage with the material and take meaning from it. They may need strategies in order to decode the odd unfamiliar word but they should be able to do so independently and without losing their thread.

Instructional level AKA warm porridge

At this level, the reader finds this text challenging - with one word in ten proving difficult - but manageable, and can read it with support. Support enables students who are reading at this more difficult level to access more sophisticated vocabulary and sentence structures.

Frustration level AKA hot porridge

At this level, the reader has difficulty with more than one word in ten, and thus finds the text frustrating to read. Students should never be asked to read texts at this level - even with support - because interrupting the text every time they struggle with a word means they grow frustrated and so lose their motivation and enthusiasm.

When working independently, students should be given texts to read that fall within their independent level. When involved in guided reading aimed at developing students' vocabulary, students should be given texts to read that fall within their instructional level. Texts which appear at a student's frustration level can still be used in class but only if they are read to them by the teacher. This helps expose student to more sophisticated vocabulary and syntax.

Reading to the class is a pleasure which should not end when students reach puberty. Students of all ages and abilities enjoy being read to and having texts read to them which are beyond their own capacities exposes students to more sophisticated vocabulary and language structures. Reading aloud also allows teachers to model their thinking, showing how they draw meaning from a text.

Developing comprehension

Comprehension - being able to read for meaning - is important because reading allows students to access the whole curriculum and opens up the world.

Comprehension, therefore, needs to be taught and not just tested. We cannot assume that our students have the comprehension skills they need in order to succeed in school and even those students who have mastered the art of decoding may need help developing more advanced strategies for constructing meaning from a text.

Many teachers, however, believe that reading a text and asking questions about its content is enough. Answering questions on a text only tests what the student has understood; it is not a means of helping them to develop a deeper understanding. In other words, asking questions may test but it does not teach comprehension. Teaching comprehension is, in many ways, the same as teaching thinking.

In order to teach comprehension, we need to: explain and demonstrate a range of comprehension strategies; guide students as they practise these strategies; and evaluate students' use of these strategies.

For example, we need to make explicit the kinds of reading strategies we experienced readers use implicitly all the time such as: making predictions, relating information in a text to our own experiences and knowledge, asking and answering questions, creating images in our minds, and continually summarising the main points.

We should use a variety of reading materials, too, including some short texts such as newspaper headlines, lists, labels, reports, text messages, instructions and so on because these are the kinds of texts that form most of our daily reading. Texts of all types and lengths can be used for teaching comprehension.

We need to teach active listening. Verbal comprehension, we

know, precedes reading comprehension and this requires active listening. Hearing is not the same as active listening. Active listening requires sustained attention, cognitive processing in the working memory, and information storage and retrieval. We can help our students to develop these skills by giving them tasks to do such as listening for specific or key information in a long speech. To help them, we need to teach them strategies - such as mnemonics, linking new information to prior knowledge, and verbal rehearsal - to remember information. We also need to return to this information later, asking students to retrieve and recall it.

Let's take a look at some specific strategies for developing comprehension before we start reading, whilst we're reading, and once we've finished reading...

Before reading
- Explore what students already know about the topic of the text.
- Relate students' own experiences to the text.
- Ask students to make predictions about the text based on the title and any illustrations, this helps build background knowledge and increases their motivation for reading.
- Ask students to tell you about any other texts they've read on the same topic.
- Explicitly teach any new vocabulary students are likely to encounter, especially words which are crucial to understanding the text.

Whilst reading
- Read most of the text - particularly important parts of it - without lots of interruptions so that students can understand the plot and structure (following a sequence of events) and so that students can attune to the written style. Asking questions before and after reading the text are more effective and less intrusive than questions asked during reading.
- Signpost the new vocabulary you taught before reading.
- Pause occasionally - where appropriate - to gauge students' reactions: ask for comments, questions and predictions.
- Teach students strategies for regaining the meaning of a text

when they begin to struggle or lose interest: e.g. reread the sentence carefully, think about what might make sense; reread the sentence before and after the one you're stuck on, look for familiar words inside or around an unfamiliar word.
- Teach students to monitor their understanding of the text by using post-it notes or page-markers. Post-it notes could be to used to: indicate a connection between the text and a prior experience or piece of knowledge, as well as between the text and another text; identify information which surprised them; and highlight something students want to ask later.

After reading
- Teach students how to identify the key words in a passage (the words that explain who, what, where, when, how or why).
- Teach students note-taking skills and other ways of summarising information such as graphic organisers (e.g. story maps, timelines, flow charts, plot profiles, etc.).
- Ask questions that help students to identify a sequence of events.
- Teach students to look out for cause and effect relationships.
- Ask students to rewrite the text in a different form: for example, from a diary to a time-line, from a set of instructions to a flow chart, from a piece of descriptive writing to a drawing.
- Teach students to use reference material such as a dictionary and thesaurus, a glossary and bibliography.

Questioning as a means of developing comprehension

Earlier I said that reading a text and asking questions about its content is a way to test rather than teach comprehension. However, that is not to say that questions do not have their place in the classroom...

As with many such strategies, the effectiveness of questioning depends on whether or not the teacher is clear about the purpose of their questions. Questions should only be used if they cause thinking and/or provide information for the teacher about what to do next. The most common model of questioning is IRE (Initiation, Response, Evaluation) but this doesn't work very well.

Instead, a better model is ABC (Agree/disagree with, Build upon, and Challenge) whereby students pass questions around the classroom. The Japanese call this technique 'neriage' - which means 'to polish' - because students polish each other's answers, refining them as they pass them around the room.

Some questions are better than others, too, because different types of question demand different levels of understanding and engage different cognitive processes...

The best questions promote higher order thinking: they are an expressive demonstration of genuine curiosity, have an inner logic, are ordered so that thinking is clarified and are a part of an ongoing dialogue. These higher-order thinking questions usually begin with 'how' or 'why' and include modal verbs like 'would', 'might', 'should', and 'could'. They promote more imaginative and complex thinking, as do questions that include aspirational words like 'imagine', 'decide', 'think', and 'believe'.

That's not to say that we should never use lower-order questions. When teaching basic factual information, asking straightforward closed questions can give students the opportunity to display the knowledge that they will build on later. These types of questions can also alert teachers to the students who have not understood essential information.

Understanding what kind of question will best develop our students' higher cognitive processing, and knowing how to phrase a question, are important skills for teachers. There are several ways in which researchers have levelled types of questions...

The speech therapist Marion Blank devised a hierarchy of questions which starts with those related to the immediate environment ('What is that?' 'What is _____ doing?') and builds to questions which involve problem solving, making predictions, finding solutions, and testing explanations ('What will happen if...?' 'What should we do now?').

Harold Bloom's Taxonomy of Educational Objectives is often used to identify different levels of questions. Bloom's taxonomy originally had six levels as follows:

1. Knowledge

2. Comprehension

3. Application

4. Analysis

5. Synthesis

6. Evaluation

Here are some example question stems using these six levels:

Knowledge:
What happened...?
How many...?
Who said...?
Name the...?
Describe what happened when...?
Who spoke to...?
What is the meaning of...?
What is...?
Is it true or false...?

Comprehension:
In your own words, write about...
Write a brief outline...?
What happened next...
Who do you think...?
Can you distinguish between...?
What differences exist between...?
Can you provide an example of...?
Can you provide a definition for...?

Application:
Could this have happened in...?
Group these items by...

What factors would you change if...?
Can you apply the method used to some experience of your own...?
What questions would you ask...?
Can you develop a set of instructions about...?

Analysis:
What might the ending have been like if...?
In what way was this similar to...?
What was the underlying theme of...?
Why did that happen...?
Can you compare...?
Can you explain what happened when...?
How is ... similar to ...?
Can you distinguish between...?
What were the motives behind...?
What was the turning point in this sequence of events...?
What was the problem with...?

Synthesis:
Can you write a poem about...?
Can you see a possible solution to...?
What would happen if...?
How many ways can you...?
Can you create a new and unusual use for...?
Can you write a recipe for...?
Can you develop a proposal which would...

Evaluation:
Is there a better solution to...?
Can you defend your position about...?
How would you have dealt with...?
What changes would you recommend for...?
How would you feel if...?
How successful is...?
What do you think about...?

Bloom's Taxonomy was updated in 2005 by Glasson and now has five which, in increasing order of sophistication, is as follows:

1. Remember

2. Comprehend

3. Apply

4. Evaluate

5. Create

Graham & Wong, (1993) developed the 3H strategy for developing students' comprehension. The 3 Hs in question are: *Here, Hidden, and Head*. Moving students through the three stages takes them from literal to deductive questions.

1. 'Here' questions are literal questions, the answers to which are apparent in the text. For example, 'What was the Stable Buck called in Of Mice and Men?

2. 'Hidden' questions require students to synthesise information from different parts of a text. For example, 'How did Curley's Wife's life change when she got married?'

3. 'Head' questions require students to use their prior knowledge in order to predict or deduce. For example, 'Do you think George ever really believed he'd own his own ranch? Why do you think that?'

The 3H strategy relies on the teacher being able to devise questions at the three different levels and use them in order to extend their students' thinking. The teacher can model the process by thinking aloud.

Here are some useful tips for asking questions in the classroom in order to develop students' comprehension:
- Make sure you word your questions clearly.
- When teaching basic factual information, use lower level

questions to check for understanding.

- When asking lower level questions, keep the pace brisk.
- Ask questions both before and after texts are read, not just whilst reading.
- Use more and more higher level questions as students get older and more developed.
- Keep wait-time to about three seconds for discussions using lower level questions but...
- Increase wait-time when asking higher-level questions, perhaps to as much as five minutes.
- Encourage students to use wait-time to talk to a partner or to write notes.

Before we more away from comprehension, let's take a look at some strategies for helping our students to develop their comprehension skills. We'll start with the practice of guided reading...

CHAPTER TEN

STRATEGIES FOR DEVELOPING COMPREHENSION

I

GUIDED READING

Guided Reading tends to be used in Early Years education and ensures young students have the support they need to read a book as independently as possible on their first attempt. However, it is an effective strategy to use in the later phases of schooling, too.

Here's how it works...

The teacher works with a small group of about four students, introducing a new text to the group. Each student has a copy of the text and they read the text independently. The teacher works with the group, observing, listening to, and assisting individual students as they read.

Guided Reading enables a teacher to:
- Match students to the appropriate texts;
- Develop, within context, students' use of effective reading strategies;
- Observe the reading strategies used by students;
- Assist students in finding meaning and enjoyment in reading;
- Develop comprehension and thinking skills; and
- Prompt the effective use of reading strategies.

Guided reading is a useful strategy for improving literacy because it helps to develop students' phonological awareness, phonics instruction, fluency, vocabulary development and comprehension - in other words, the essential components of reading instruction and those that have been identified as being the most effective approaches to teaching students to read. Let's take a look at how guided reading helps develop some of these components of reading...

Phonological Awareness
Guided reading helps students to develop greater phonemic awareness and a greater awareness of words (including rhyme, syllables, and onset and rime - see above) because the teacher can encourage students to monitor their reading accuracy and solve the mystery of new words using phonemic awareness and letter-sound relationships. The teacher can encourage students to take words apart and split them into sounds. Letters can be studied and connected to sounds.

Phonics Instruction
Guided reading helps students to learn the relationship between sounds and letters because, as new words are read, the teacher can encourage students to take the words apart, adding, deleting or substituting letters. The teacher can also encourage students to use letter-sound information to help solve the mystery of unfamiliar words.

Fluency
Guided reading helps students develop the ability to read quickly and naturally because the teacher can provide opportunities for students to read aloud and can model fluent reading by reading

and thinking aloud. Texts with rhyme, rhythm, repetition, and direct speech can be chosen for guided reading because these will facilitate fluent reading. The teacher can encourage students to engage in discussions about the texts and students can work with the teacher to explore the meaning of the text.

Vocabulary Instruction
Guided reading helps students to understand new words because the teacher can introduce new and unusual words and encourage students to discuss them. The teacher can also encourage students to substitute interesting words when talking about the text.

Comprehension
Guided reading helps students to make meaning of what is being read because, as students read, the teacher can encourage them to talk and think about what they know about the topic. The teacher can also encourage students to discuss, recount or summarise the text after they have completed it.

In order for guided reading to be successful, the learning environment must be organised. For example, whilst the teacher works with the guided reading group, other students must also be engaged in meaningful reading. The best reading practice occurs when students read continuous texts at their instructional level (see above). This might mean continuing to read texts which were started during an earlier guided reading session but now doing so independently.

An organised learning environment also means having ready access to a broad and rich range of literature and other high quality texts of all types and lengths. This might be a case of developing your own classroom library or requesting book boxes from the school library. An organised learning environment extends beyond the classroom door and indeed beyond the school gates. It requires an effective home-school agreement, a partnership between teachers and parents which encourages students to take texts home from school to practise and to read to their parents. As above, the texts which students take home should be familiar and need to be at an instructional, easy level.

The books used during guided reading are ideal 'take-home' books as they provide students with an opportunity to practise their developing reading strategies, practise the skills they have been learning in the classroom, and be successful readers.

II

OTHER STRATEGIES

Language is a sequence of words linked together by grammar. What more can teachers do to help students understand what they read? Here is a further list of useful strategies for helping to develop students' comprehension skills...

1. Sit students in pairs or small groups and ask them to talk about something they are reading or have read - without intervention from adults.

2. Take students to the library and encourage them to borrow anything that they want.

3. Plan opportunities for students to read a book, or books, quietly and on their own.

4. Encourage students to collect printed material so that they can browse it, sort it and re-sort it. For example, students might collect comics, annuals, magazines, second hand books etc.

5. Encourage students to ask you questions about something they've read in a newspaper or on the internet, or heard on TV. Regardless of whether you know the answer, say you're not sure of the answer then ask the students how they can find out, where they'd find the answer. Once the answer has been located, read it together and discuss it as well as the process of finding it.

6. Write open questions which have a number of different plausible answers to be discussed. For example, ask whether or not something is fair, or what students think about a character and what they have done.

7. Ask students to write prequels or sequels to a book they've read.

8. Encourage and help students to talk about other books, films and TV programmes which the book they're reading might remind them of.

9. Help students to talk about events in their own life (or in the lives of people they know) which they are reminded of by the book they're reading.

10. Plan opportunities for students - working in pairs or small groups independent of the teacher - to read texts aloud. Encourage them to direct each other so that they divide the text into equal parts. Ask them to think of ways they could improve their performance.

11. Ask students to think of alternative titles for the chapter, poem or book that they've read.

12. Ask students to make book recommendations: discuss amongst the class what might be the best ways of recommending a book or magazine or comic to someone else. What are helpful things for someone to know if a book is good or not?

13. Discuss the ideas or messages contained within books, films, and TV programmes. Use the example of the 'moral' at the end of an Aesop fable.

14. In poems and stories, people and creatures can represent things other than what they are. For example, in Little Red Riding Hood, the wolf could represent 'danger' (and, as we've seen above, Goldilocks could represent 'wanton thief'). Ask students questions like, 'What kind of danger does the wolf represent?'

To conclude...

SOME READING QUICK WINS:

- Teach the reading skills needed in your subject – e.g. skimming, scanning, analysis, and research.
- Present hand-outs in an attractive and accessible way, taking account of students' reading ages
- Include a list of key words at the start of hand-outs
- Include a 'big picture' question or statement at the start of hand-outs which helps students to understand why they are reading it and what help it will provide
- Ensure that the questions you ask about a text move beyond straightforward comprehension towards exploratory talk involving 'why' and 'how' questions

CHAPTER ELEVEN

STRATEGIES FOR TEACHING READING

The following reading strategies - the things we accomplished readers do implicitly all the time - need to be taught explicitly (making the invisible visible) in order to help students become more effective readers:

1. Strategies for helping students to decode texts and read for meaning

Skim – teach students how to skim a text for when they need only a general idea of what the text is about in order to determine whether or not it is going to be useful. Teach them to run their eyes quickly over the text. Teach them to look at headlines, headings, subheadings, titles, the opening lines of paragraphs and words that signal a new point is being made.

Scan – teach students how to find a specific piece of information quickly. Teach them to glance quickly down the text for key words. Teach them to run a finger down the middle of the page as they read in order to focus where they move their eyes.

Read closely – teach students how to explore the details in the text. Teach them to read all the words in a short section. Teach them to read and reread difficult sections, revising their interpretations each time. Teach them to use text marking in order to identify key points and paraphrase what the writer is saying.

Read continuously – teach students how to understand a full account of something. Teach them to read all the words, but to read some sections more quickly.

See images – teach students how to visualise what the writer is describing. Teach them to think about what pictures they can see of the characters, the settings and the action.

Hear voices – teach students how to think about whose voices they hear and how these change. Teach them to think about how the central characters sound and the sound effects of all the action. What can you hear while you read?

Establish a relationship with the narrator – teach students how to think about the narrator – the person speaking in the text. Teach them how to identify who the narrator is. Ask them questions like, 'Do you like her/him?' and 'What would you say to him/her if she/he were in the room?'

Establish a relationship with the writer – teach students how to hear the writer's voice. Teach them how to identify the author hiding behind a narrator or character or speaking directly to the reader. Ask them questions like, 'What do you think the writer is trying to say to you?'

Predict what will happen – teach students how to use what they know about a text to suggest what they think will happen next. Ask them questions like, 'Can you explain why?' and 'What evidence have you got?'

Relate to a text – teach students how to relate to a text by asking them questions like, "How does this remind you of something you have done in your life or something you have seen or heard about?' and 'How does this make you feel about the events in the text?'

2. Strategies for helping students to understand a text, to select and retrieve information or ideas from texts, and to use quotation / make reference to a text

Use PEE paragraphs - teach students how to write an analysis of a text by making a point, supporting that point with evidence, and explaining the quote.

Scan the text for the correct information - teach students how to present information as a series of bullet points using their own words.

Summarise a text - teach students how to write a short synopsis of a text, perhaps by writing down 3 bullet points that summarise what the text is about. Teach them how to reduce a text down to five sentences, then five words and then one word.

Skim a text - teach students how to read a text for no more than 20 seconds and identify which parts of it caught their attention.

Close read a text - teach students how to read a text closely and identify from each paragraph or section, a sentence that makes the main point.

Identify bias - teach students how to highlight all the facts in one colour and all the opinions in another colour in order to ascertain whether or not the text is biased.

Restructure key information in a different format - teach students how to convert a text into a spider diagram, a set of bullet points, a time line, a flow diagram, etc.

Compare texts - teach students how to read two or more texts and make a list of the similarities and differences between the texts.

3. Strategies for helping students to deduce, infer or interpret information, events or ideas from texts

Infer – teach students how to look for what is implied (suggested) rather than what is explicit (stated/obvious). Teach them to read between the lines to find the meaning. Teach them to look at the words and how they are organised in order to see the writers' different meanings.

Deduce - teach students how to use evidence in a text to work out what is meant by it, filling in gaps and making links between ideas.

Respond to statements related to a text - teach students how to infer if the statements are:
- literally true (the writer actually states them)
- inferentially true (the writer doesn't state them but the reader can work out from the text that they are true)
- incorrect (there is no evidence to back up the statements from the text)

Empathise with a character - teach students how to imagine they are in the same situation as the characters or people. Ask questions like, 'What would you do?' and 'How would you feel?'

Skim read extracts - teach students how to speculate about the type of text they come from and what type of audience the text is intended for.

4. Strategies for helping students to identify and comment on the structure and organisation of texts, including grammatical and presentational features

Read the text closely - teach students how to divide a text into sections and give each section/paragraph a subtitle or key word.

Scan the text - teach students how to pick out key features that

124

make it clear whether or not the text is fiction or non-fiction. Teach them to analyse features of presentation and language.

Skim the text - teach students how to identify any features of the layout which the writer uses to emphasise key points (e.g. bold font, underlined text, italics, bullet points, etc.)

Use graphic organisers - teach students how to represent aspects of a text in visual form. For example:
- **Trace the moments of tension** - teach students how to create an 'emotion' or 'tension' graph for the events of the text. Teach them to plot the tension in central characters by mapping quotations relating to events on the vertical axis and quotations relating to characters' emotions on the horizontal axis.
- **Trace narrative structure** - teach students how to draw a graph to show the structure of a text and the changing levels of humour, tension and drama.
- **Trace events and ideas** - teach students how to produce a narrative map/flow diagram of the events and ideas in a text and how to log the structure onto a grid e.g. a point/evidence grid, a cause/effect grid, or a argument/counter-argument grid.

Identify links - teach students how to analyse the whole text structure. Teach them to identify how links are made between paragraphs and within paragraphs.

5. Strategies for helping students to explain and comment on a writers' use of language

Hear a reading voice - teach students how to think about the following features:
- the use of pronouns
- the type of punctuation used
- the 'voice' of the writer
- the type of advice given.

Identify the writer and the audience - teach students how to pick out words or phrases which provide clues as to the identity, point of view, and motivation of the writer, and to the identity of the intended audience.

Identify persuasive techniques - teach students how to identify the techniques the writer uses in order to persuade the audience to their point of view, e.g. the opening statement, the use of pronouns - 'we' and 'us', the use of rhetorical questions, the use of repetition and metaphorical language, etc.

Identify emotive language - teach students how to scan a text and locate examples of emotive language. Teach them to comment on why the writer has used them and what they hoped to achieve.

Identify the writer's tone of voice - teach students how to close read a text in order to identify the tone of voice it is written in. For example, the presence of irony, self-deprecation, exaggeration and rhetorical devices might suggest a humorous tone and the presence of colloquialisms and asides (parenthesises) might suggest an informal tone.

6. Strategies for helping students to identify and comment on a writers' purpose and viewpoint, and the overall effect of the text on the reader

Analyse feelings - teach students to be aware of and note down their feelings whilst they read a text and then try to explain why they felt that way.

Identify the narrative voice - teach students to identify whether a text is written in the first or third person. Teach them to analyse and comment on the effect this choice has on the reader.

Ask questions of a text - teach students how to question the effect the ideas/arguments/viewpoints in the text have on the reader. Teach them to consider why the writer has used them.

Ask questions of the writer - teach students how to question the writer's choices of presentation and language, as well as the writer's feelings, views and attitudes. Teach them to speculate about what his/her responses would be.

Establish a relationship with the writer - teach students how to identify clues in a text about the writer's attitude to the subject/person he/she is writing about. Teach them to consider the language the writer has used to describe the person/subject.

7. Strategies for helping students to relate texts to their social, cultural and historical contexts and literary tradition

Compare texts from the past with the present - teach students how to identify things from a text that are different to the present day. Teach them to ask if anything has changed and, if so, why.

Identify and decode old words - teach students how to identify words which we no longer use and to read backwards and forwards in order to try understand what they mean. Teach them to identify how sentence structures may have changed over time, too.

Identify and decode words from other cultures - teach students how to pick out words and phrases that tell them the text is written about a different country or culture. Teach them to work out the meaning by looking at the rest of the text or by using reference texts. Teach students how to investigate the ways in which different cultures/countries use different spellings or grammar.

Use visual organisers - teach students how to produce a chart to record ways in which language has changed over time or is different. One column could be 'Word from text' and the other column 'Modern Meaning/Translation'.

PART FOUR

WRITING

CHAPTER TWELVE

AN INTRODUCTION TO WRITING

Writing has traditionally been one of the weakest areas of literacy teaching. All too often teachers assume that imparting knowledge – making sure our students know stuff – is enough. In reality, of course, the most common and effective means by which most knowledge is assessed - whether that be in exams or through controlled assessments and coursework, class and homework - is through students' writing.

Writing, therefore, needs to be taught by every teacher who uses writing as a means of assessment.

This is not a case of asking teachers to do anything technical or beyond their comfort zones: it's asking teachers merely to help their students to write like a designer or artist or musician or scientist. It is, in other words, about teaching and learning, our core purpose.

According to Hillocks, teaching the key ingredients of writing involves the teacher using three broad approaches:

- Presentational: setting tasks and success criteria.

- Process: giving students some choice of task and developing writing through the use of drafts and peer assessment strategies (e.g. gallery critique).

- Environmental: using strategies to help students to write better.

The quality of writing is usually better when it emerges from reading. That doesn't mean simply displaying a good model of a text on the whiteboard. Teaching writing is more active than that. It involves:

1. Modelling: the teacher sharing information about a text.

2. Joint construction: the teacher and students working together to create a text collaboratively.

3. Independent construction: students constructing a text in a new genre independently of others, albeit with the support of peers and the teacher.

4. Active teaching of vocabulary and sentence structures.

However, here's a word of warning: we can't teach writing simply by showing model texts, even if we annotate them to show what makes them work. Instead, we teach writing by writing.

If we simply show writing exemplars on the board, we are in danger of giving students the mistaken impression that writing is a product rather than a process. Students need to see that writing is something that involves making decisions and, for that matter, making mistakes. Students need to see their teacher – and that means their teachers in all subjects – writing. This might involve:

Contemplating the 'what' and the 'how' of a text – what is its purpose and who is its audience? The answers to those questions will affect how the text is written both in terms of its language and its presentation.

Examining the conventions of a text – again, this is both in terms of language (formality, style, sentence structure, etc.) and presentation (paragraphs, sequence, bullet points, images, etc.).

Demonstrating how the text might be written - this involves students observing the teacher as they 'think aloud', explaining the decisions they take. For example, thinking aloud might sound like this: "I need to write this like a historian would write it. It will need to be in the third person, so 'he/she' and 'they' not 'I'. It will need to be formal not colloquial but not too stuffy either, it has to be accessible to a wide audience. Now talk to your partner about what your first sentence might say. Then we'll listen to some of your examples and compare them with what I write down." This articulation moves from modelling to composing to assessment.

Writing a text whilst providing a running commentary - this involves explaining the decisions that are made, and how words are selected and rejected.

Let's look at some common features of different text types that will help teachers of all subjects to know what to look for and what to teach...

Instructions - such as a recipe or a guide to assembling a piece of furniture - are usually written in the passive voice ('place part A on top of part B and insert screw 1') or written in the second person ('you take part A and place it on top of part B, then you insert screw 1'). Instructions tend to start with the aim - in a recipe, this would be a description of the dish you are about to create. Next, there is often a list of ingredients or components that are required - perhaps bullet-pointed. This is followed by the method: a list of what you need to do - sequenced chronologically, perhaps using a numbered list. This will be in the present tense and make use of imperative verbs (commands).

Recounts are texts which tell the audience about something, giving an account of an event or experience. Recounts - certainly those which appear in newspapers - tend to be written using the inverted pyramid structure which means they begin with the key facts - answering the questions Who? What? Where? and When? - and then provide background information. Recounts tend to be written in chronological order, perhaps with connectives related to time such as 'firstly' and 'secondly', 'next' and 'then'. They tend to be written in the past tense. They tend to be written in an active voice (he/she/they). In the case of newspaper articles and reports, they are written in the third person (he/she); in the case of autobiographies and travelogues, they are written in the first person (I).

Discursive writing articulates a discussion or argument. It tends to be fluent and expansive. Discursive writing usually outlines the main arguments for and against an action, providing evidence to support one side of the argument and perhaps even supporting both sides of the debate. Having articulated both views, it will come to a conclusion. Discursive writing tends to be written in the active voice using connectives to show debate such as those which compare and contrast (similarly, conversely, however, therefore). Discursive writing can be written in either the past or the present tense but tends to be written in the third person. It makes use of rhetorical devices such as rhetorical questions, repetition, alliteration, exaggeration, and so on.

Persuasive writing presents an argument by expressing an opinion and supporting each point with evidence. It might present a biased account without acknowledging an alternative view or it might present both sides of a debate before concluding which side of the argument is right and why. If it presents the counter-argument, it might challenge each point, perhaps with selective evidence. The conclusion of the argument will be summarised at the end. Persuasive writing is usually written in the present tense and makes good use of rhetorical devices and emotive language. It might use connectives which show the relationship between sides of the argument such as 'therefore' and 'however', and 'because' and 'consequently'.

Analytical writing is - as you would expect - that which analyses something, carrying out a detailed examination of the elements or structure of something, perhaps by separating it into its constituent parts. Analytical writing tends to be thematically structured rather than chronological. It tends to be written in the third person and in an active voice. It can be written in either the past or present tense. It will contain numerous facts, providing evidence for any assertions made.

Reports are usually written in the present tense using formal language. They are often written in the first person and make good use of action verbs as well as non-emotive descriptive language. Reports tend to be non-chronological - using the inverted pyramid explained above.

Evaluative writing assesses the effectiveness of something by weighing up the strengths and weaknesses, pros and cons. It tends to be written in the first person but can be either past, present or future tense. It uses the active voice. It often makes use of bullet-points and sub-headings to organise materials succinctly and logically, as well as connectives to show the balance between two sides such as 'however'.

Writing which explains something tends to follow a logical sequence, perhaps chronological. It might use connectives which support the sequential nature of the text such as 'firstly', 'secondly', 'thirdly' or 'next' and 'then'. It tends to use the present tense and be written in the third person with an active voice. It makes use of commands - imperative verbs such as 'take the container' and 'pour the water'.

Writing which informs tends to be impersonal, using third person. It is factual and clear - avoiding opinion and ambiguity. Sentences and paragraphs tend to be short. It tends to use connectives which show the sequence of events or cause and effect.

To conclude...

SOME WRITING QUICK WINS:
- Model how to write the first paragraph of an essay/evaluation/description, etc.
- Teach the essential connectives of writing such as however, because, as, so, although, while, despite, on the other hand.
- Encourage students to use short sentences at the start and end of paragraphs

CHAPTER THIRTEEN

STRATEGIES FOR TEACHING WRITING

1. Strategies for helping students to write imaginative, interesting and thoughtful texts

Share high quality exemplars (full texts and extracts) with students to explore different ways of writing.

Model the writing process for students, perhaps by completing every writing task you give to students on the Smartboard or by writing a text collaboratively as a class.

Use visual stimuli to inspire students' writing, e.g. images of people, places, objects, etc.

Use speaking and listening activities as an introduction to writing tasks, e.g. role play, hot seating, debate, discussion, etc.

Provide a range of planning and writing frames for students to use.

2. Strategies for helping students to produce texts which are appropriate to their audience and purpose

Use a sequence for teaching writing such as this:
- Establish clear aims – APT (Audience, Purpose, Technique)
- Provide examples of the text type being produced
- Explore the main features of presentation and language in the example text. Read and discuss word, sentence and text-level features.
- Define the conventions of the text type being produced – agree on the main 'ingredients' for this kind of writing
- Demonstrate how a text is written by modelling the thought process (think aloud)
- Compose a text (or the introduction to a text) together as a class
- Scaffold students' first attempts – e.g. use writing frames, lists of key words, the beginnings of sentences
- Provide time for students to write independently
- Review key learning

Annotate the task to make sure students know who they are writing for, (audience), why they are writing (purpose), and what type of writing they will be doing (technique).

Try, wherever possible, to provide real-life tasks for genuine audiences - research has shown that all writers perform better when they draw on real experiences and have a clear sense of who they are writing for. Use APT as a checklist for audience, purpose, and technique.

Use card sort activities whereby students match up examples of texts with the appropriate audience, purpose, and techniques.

3. Strategies for helping students to sequence and structure information, ideas, and events effectively

Model the planning process for students, introducing a variety of writing frames including templates for note-making.

Teach the main features of different text types (e.g. instructions are chronological)

Make explicit a sequence for planning which might include:
- write initial thoughts and ideas on Post-it notes or cards
- identify key words or phrases which need to be included
- draft the topic sentences and/or sub-headings
- organise these sentences/sub-headings into a logical sequence

Use visual organisers such as flowcharts, mind maps, graphs and tables, in order to support the planning and writing process.

4. Strategies for helping students to construct paragraphs and to make links within and between paragraphs

Paragraph Organisation:
- Share a paragraphed text with students and ask them to identify why each paragraph starts where it does.
- Share a paragraphed text with students and ask them to give each paragraph a sub-heading which summarises the subject of the paragraph.
- Give students a card sort activity: ask them to match cards which have bullet-pointed information on them with cards which have headings on them. Then ask students to use each pair of cards to write a paragraph.
- Share a text with students which doesn't have any paragraph breaks in it then ask them to identify where a new paragraph should start and why.

Paragraph Structure:
- Share a paragraph with students and ask them how the writer must have determined in which order the sentences should have appeared.
- Give students a paragraph to read which has had its sentences cut up into strips. Ask them to organise the sentences back into a paragraph and explain how the paragraph is structured (e.g. by chronology), what clues helped them complete the

task, (e.g. sequencing connectives) and why they chose that sequence.
- Give students a cloze exercise to do: share a paragraph with students which has had all its connectives removed. Ask students to identify how the paragraph is structured and suggest appropriate connectives to fill the gaps.

Paragraph Links:
- Share a text with students and ask them to identify how the paragraphs have been linked together.
- Give students a card sort to do: half the cards are connectives and half describe their function. Ask students to match the connective with its function, e.g. 'Consequently' is matched with 'Cause and Effect', and 'However' is matched with 'Compare and Contrast'.
- Give students a text to read which has had its paragraphs cut up and jumbled. Ask them to use the connectives and links as clues in order to correctly re-form the text.
- Teach students how to write in PEE paragraphs - point, evidence, explanation. Later, add L = links (PEEL).

5. Strategies for helping students to vary their sentences for clarity, purpose and effect

Encourage students to vary the openings of their sentences. For example, write a text in which at least one sentence:
- Starts with a verb ending in ing...
- Starts with a verb ending in ed...
- Starts with an adverb ending ly...
- Starts with a preposition e.g. over, at, on,
- Starts with an adjective e.g. Cold and weary they sank ...

Encourage students to vary the lengths of their sentences. For example, write a text in which there is at least one:
- Simple sentence
- Compound sentence
- Complex sentence

Encourage students to vary the purpose of their sentences. For example, write a text in which there is at least one:
- Declarative sentence
- Exclamative sentence
- Inquisitive sentence
- Imperative sentence

Encourage students to use a range of connectives which go beyond 'and' and to use connectives in order to:
- Combine sentences
- Start sentences (with a comma)
- Link sentences and paragraphs
- Express thinking more clearly

Give students a complex sentence and ask them to move the clauses around to create different effects and emphasis.

Teach students how sentences can vary for purpose and effect, e.g. using lots of short sentences creates tension whereas using lots of long, periodic sentences creates suspense.

6. Strategies for helping students to write with accurate syntax and punctuation in phrases, clauses and sentences

Give students a series of sentences written in 'hangman' style with underscores and punctuation but no letters and ask them identify the sentence types.

Get students to use sequencing when reviewing and previewing learning to get used to using time prepositions:
- Before last lesson, I knew…
- During last lesson, I learnt…
- Since last lesson, I found out…
- By the end of this lesson I want to know…

Give students a text and ask them to highlight the main and subordinate clauses in different colours and then explain the effect.

Give students three complex sentences which make different uses of main clauses and subordinate clauses (main + subordinate, subordinate + main, and main + embedded subordinate) and ask them to identify the different clauses and explain their answers.

Give students a 'punctuation role' to play in a piece of direct speech (speech marks, comma, capital letter, final punctuation mark). Read out a sentence aloud and tell the students to stand at the front of the class in the order in which their designated punctuation occurs.

Play punctuation bingo whereby the teacher reads aloud a series of sentences and students cross out the appropriate punctuation mark on their bingo cards.

7. Strategies for helping students to select appropriate and effective vocabulary

Teach the use of synonyms – identify a word in a sentence and ask students to think of a list of alternative words which have the same meaning. This will improve their vocabulary and the quality of their writing. Focus on providing alternatives for high frequency words such as 'said' and 'walked'.

Get students to play word detectives using thesauruses and dictionaries to find the meaning of words.

Play 'Call My Bluff' by giving students several definitions for unusual words and ask them to guess the correct meaning.

Create lists of words that show varying degrees of meaning and order them from low to high, e.g. from boiling to tepid.

Ask students to think of powerful adjectives to describe different things such as a movement or a noise.

8. Strategies for helping students to use the correct spelling

Teach students how to:
- Break words into sounds/phonemes (p-a-r-t-y)
- Break words into syllables (dem-oc-ra-cy)
- Break words into an affix and root word (un + happy)
- Use a mnemonic (Big Elephants Can Always Upset Small Elephants for BECAUSE or one Collar two Sleeves for neCeSSary)
- Refer to different words in the same family (chemical, chemist, chemistry)
- Over-articulate silent or hidden letters (Wed-nes-day)
- Identify words within words (GUM in argument)
- Refer to a word's etymology / history (tri = three, pod = foot)
- Use analogy (through, rough, enough)
- Use a key word (I'm – to remember a apostrophe can replace a missing letter)
- Apply spelling rules (hopping = short vowel sound, hoping = long vowel)
- Learn by sight (look-say-cover-write-check)
- Use a 'mind palace' of visual memories (recall images, colour, font)

CHAPTER FOURTEEN

SOME GENERAL 'QUICK WINS'

Before we move on, let's take a look at a few general pieces of advice for developing speaking and listening, reading, and writing skills...

In classrooms and corridors
- Display subject key words
- Display annotated examples of what high quality work looks like
- Display and reinforce the learning objective for every lesson to ensure all learners know what they are expected to learn and how they will demonstrate it

PART FIVE

LEADING LITERACY

CHAPTER FIFTEEN

WHAT IS EFFECTIVE LITERACY TEACHING?

I'm going to return to Sinek's golden circle but place a different spin on it this time...

The teaching of literacy has to be systematic, which is to say that literacy skills must be taught in a planned and logical sequence. Literacy teaching must be informed by the assessment of student needs as well as a deep knowledge of the curriculum. Effective literacy teachers plan how they will monitor and assess their students' learning, differentiate their teaching practice, and gradually release responsibility for learning to students.

Let's take a closer look at how this might work... let's start with why...

WHY: Assessment

Effective literacy teachers use assessment *for*, *as* and *of* learning.

Assessment for learning: teachers focus on the gap between how a student is performing currently, and how they need to perform in the future in order to achieve (and ideally exceed) their target, and identify what they need to do in order to close the gap. Armed with this information, teachers provide feedback using thoughtful questions, careful listening and reflective responses, and they explicitly teach the things students need to develop most.

Assessment as learning: teachers and students identify and reflect on their own evidence of learning, help to set their own learning goals, and engage in self- and peer-assessment activities.

Assessment of learning: teachers use evidence of learning (or performance) to make judgments about a student's achievement against his/her targets and/or the assessment criteria.

HOW: Pedagogy

Effective literacy teachers understand pedagogy and practice and use this to maximise students' engagement in lessons as well as to develop students' literacy knowledge, skills and understanding. They are clear about what they want students to learn and the best ways to help them learn it. They are aware of their students' prior knowledge and future needs and use this information to engage them in relevant and challenging work. They ensure that their pedagogy enables all students to engage with and achieve the intended outcome. They monitor the effectiveness of schemes of work and lesson plans and adapt them as required in order to ensure all students' achieve the intended learning outcomes. They carefully adapt and modify the degree to which students need additional support as students begin to gain control and become more independent learners.

WHAT: Curriculum

Effective literacy teachers draw on their understanding of the English language and on the literacy demands of their curriculum. They understand what they need to teach and the levels of attainment that are required of their students.

As I've said before - yes, I know, I'm starting to repeat myself now - literacy teaching is about making the implicit explicit, the invisible visible... In other words, teachers are most effective in teaching literacy when they carefully unpack how the English language system works, why language choices are made, and how we can use language in powerful ways. They explicitly explain, model, and scaffold the thinking and activities required of students in order to achieve their intended outcomes.

This process can helpfully be divided into six steps:

- Share the intended learning outcomes with students

- Revisit and review students' prior learning

- Demonstrate and model new learning

- Support and facilitate students as they practice their new learning

- Provide opportunities for students to practice and apply their learning independently

- Provide ongoing feedback and facilitate the self-assessment of new learning
  Before we

CHAPTER SIXTEEN

A WHOLE SCHOOL APPROACH

As we have seen, the purpose of teaching literacy is to enable every student to meet the language and literacy demands of the whole school curriculum.

According to Gavelek et al (2000), the most effective way of teaching literacy is to integrate it on three levels:

- *Within literacy:* teachers connect the aspects of a balanced literacy curriculum so that each aspect is linked. For example, writing takes place in response to reading and watching something; vocabulary and spelling are taught as a part of reading and writing activities not just discretely.

- *Across learning areas:* teachers explicitly support students to develop, practice and apply literacy skills and knowledge across subjects. For example, teachers explicitly teach how explanation texts in, say, Science and History work.

- *Within the community:* teachers support students in applying their literacy knowledge for relevant social purposes within their communities. For example, students are taught how to use their literacy learning in order to construct a safe social networking page.

In short, if our students' levels of literacy are to be improved, then we must adopt a whole school approach; it is not enough to teach literacy only in English lessons. Literacy must be threaded through the whole curriculum and be connected to students' lives beyond the school gates.

If we are to successfully embed literacy across the curriculum, we will need an agreed and coherent whole-school approach and this can only happen if every member of staff in a school works together to develop and enact consistent literacy teaching. This requires a firm commitment from senior leaders and a relentless drive by the literacy coordinator.

So what does a whole-school approach look like? It has the following ingredients:
- an agreed focus and direction for literacy improvement
- a shared understanding, commitment and language for literacy assessment and instruction
- a consistent and coherent implementation of curriculum and pedagogy across year groups and subject areas
- a collective action that uses data and evidence to drive instruction, interventions and resources
- collaborative professional learning which builds teachers' capacity to refine literacy practices
- differentiated teaching and learning which supports each student to achieve their targets

The world's highest performing schools show that success occurs when teachers have high expectations, a shared vision, and a collective belief in their ability to make a difference to young people's live. A coherent whole school approach to literacy, therefore, requires all the staff in a school to reach an agreement about what they expect students to achieve and what they expect the teaching of literacy to achieve. They also need to agree 'what' aspects of literacy they will teach, 'how' they will teach each aspect, and 'when' (i.e. in what order and at what stage of students' development/schooling) they will teach each aspect. A whole school approach requires these agreements in order to progress towards a vision that ensures successful outcomes for every student in the school.

The following are good indicators that you've achieved a whole-school approach:

Literacy teaching is *coherent*: There is a whole school vision and policy, and clear expectations in each subject which support literacy improvement for students.

Literacy teaching is *consistent*: All the staff in the school - teaching and support - have a common language, a shared understanding of and a commitment to enact the school's agreed vision.

Literacy teaching is *responsive*: All the staff in the school develop their expertise in order to enact and apply the school's vision and respond to the literacy needs of individual students.

Literacy teaching is *effective*: The whole school works together to continuously review, refine and improve its teaching of literacy in response to student achievement and other evidence.

A successful whole school approach to literacy development also requires:

Effective leadership

There is an increasing body of evidence to confirm that not only does leadership matter, but it is second only to the quality of teaching in the factors that improve learner outcomes.

Therefore, the best leaders of literacy work tirelessly to ensure that there is a coherent and consistent approach to high quality literacy teaching and learning. They articulate a clear vision for literacy learning and make explicit what a school's teaching priorities are. They also build a cohesive professional culture which seeks to develop literacy capacities and improves performance. They build their own knowledge and the knowledge of others and share expertise. Literacy leaders take strategic actions for improvement as informed by data and evidence. Finally, they are committed to ongoing learning for all.

Quality teaching

Quality literacy teaching is the responsibility of all the staff in a school. Quality literacy teaching is about creating a literacy-rich, well-organised learning environment which is safe and inclusive. It is about ensuring that literacy learning is differentiated, explicit and effective because it is responsive to the needs of all students. Quality literacy teaching is also about planning the development of literacy skills and understandings across the curriculum - in other words, knowing the literacy demands of the curriculum and explicitly and systematically teaching literacy in a balanced and integrated way. It is about ensuring that teachers can and do make a difference on a daily basis to students' achievements, in part by skilfully using assessments to plan and differentiate literacy learning in response to students' needs. Finally, it is about providing students with regular and personalised formative feedback about their learning which gives them a clear understanding of the outcomes required and how to achieve them.

Challenged and engaged students

Students are challenged and engaged when their literacy knowledge and skills are developed within a relevant and genuine context. Challenged and engaged students will be able to listen, read, view, speak, write and create increasingly complex and sophisticated texts across a range of text types with accuracy, fluency and purpose. Challenged and engaged learners will be able to apply their emerging knowledge of English confidently, effectively and critically in a range of contexts. They will have the ability to use English in powerful and effective ways in order to make decisions.

Helping students to become challenged and engaged is about knowing and valuing every student and using their prior knowledge, culture, experience, interests and skills to inform planning and teaching. Challenge and engagement occurs best when students are provided with rich, purposeful tasks that are placed within relevant and meaningful contexts.

As a result, students will become effective users of literacy - in other words, they'll be able to apply their language learning confidently and competently in a range of real life contexts. Students will become effective inquirers, too - this means they'll be able to use their language learning for a range of purposes in order to engage with others and explore their own thinking. Students will become effective risk-takers - in other words, they'll be able to set high expectations for themselves and review their own learning. Students will become effective decision-markers, too - this means they'll be able to use language critically to negotiate with and influence others.

A planned literacy curriculum

The teaching of literacy needs to be planned in such a way as to ensure there are continuing and progressive opportunities for students to develop their literacy skills. This means personalised teaching that's targeted to an individual student's literacy needs and having a high standard of achievement for all students. The literacy curriculum needs to be responsive to students' needs, monitor students' progress, and communicate clear expectations of achievement. It needs to provide individuals with challenge and support, including targeted interventions where necessary.

Working with stakeholders

Working closely with parents and carers as well as the wider community will help develop a shared responsibility for literacy learning, resulting in improved student outcomes, attendance and behaviour. Any such partnerships need to be built on trust and respect. When they work, partnerships provide students with a link between learning at home and at school, increasing parents' understanding of the role they must play in the lives of students. This involves creating regular, structured opportunities for parents and the community to be involved in school life, ensuring communication is two-way, genuine, and regular.

Good use of data and research

Data and other forms of evidence, including quality research, should be used in order to personalise teaching. Using data provides a means of monitoring, analysing and informing improvement decisions. It provides an opportunity to review the effectiveness of literacy teaching and can be used as a basis for developing the curriculum. By using data, teachers can monitor students' progress and school leaders can monitor the effectiveness of their whole school approach to literacy. For this to work, schools need to ensure they have systems in place which strategically collect and analyse data against a number of measures and need systems for ensuring that data informs the school's priorities. Teaching staff need to regularly engage with and apply contemporary research and professional learning.

PART SIX

PUTTING IT INTO PRACTICE

CHAPTER SEVENTEEN

CASE STUDY 1:
THE WRITING REVOLUTION

So much for the theory, now let's take a peek at what effective literacy teaching looks like in practice...

I'm going to invent a school - let's call it Literary High - and talk you through what the teachers and leaders at this school did in order to embed literacy across the curriculum. The ideas I'm going to share may herald from an imaginary school but they have all been tried and tested in real schools.

*

Having attempted numerous interventions in order to raise attainment, school leaders at Literacy High realised that the failure of students to get better exam results was not because they lacked intelligence, it was because they lacked the ability to comprehend texts and construct arguments. An analysis of students' writing found that students could write using simple sentences but could not do what accomplished writers do: namely, use coordinating conjunctions to link and expand on simple ideas. The best writing contains complex sentences that rely on subordinate clauses and signal a shift from one idea to another. Students, it seemed, did not know how to use some basic parts of speech. They lacked an understanding of how language worked. For example, they did not know that key information in a sentence does not always appear at the beginning.

To combat this skills shortage, Literacy High decided to develop a new curriculum built around analytical writing which placed an intense focus, across nearly every academic subject, on teaching the skills that underlie good analytical writing. Literacy High called it the Writing Revolution...

What's the Writing Revolution? I hear you cry. Well, I'm glad you asked...

The Writing Revolution - which would not be unfamiliar to nuns who taught in Catholic schools in the 1950s - is when students are explicitly taught how to turn ideas into simple sentences and how to construct complex sentences from simple sentences by answering three question prompts: **but, because,** and **so.** They are instructed on how to use appositional clauses to vary the way their sentences begin. Later in the programme, they are taught how to recognise sentence fragments, how to identify the main idea in a paragraph, and how to form an argument of their own.

The idea behind this approach is the belief that thinking, speaking, and reading comprehension are interconnected and can be reinforced through good writing instruction. As such, nearly every lesson at Literacy High is dedicated to teaching essay-writing in each subject area. In Physics, for example, a lesson which focuses on the focal length of different shaped lenses is followed by a worksheet which asks students to explain why a thicker lens would produce a shorter focal length. Their explanation should make use of subordinating clauses (e.g. students must start at least one sentence with the word 'Although').

When speaking, students are given a series of prompts that include the following:

"I agree/disagree with ___ because ..."
"I have a different opinion ..."
"I have something to add ..."
"Can you explain your answer?"

Later, students are taught how to plan an introductory paragraph then how to write main body paragraphs. Homework tasks become more difficult - moving from 'Write a letter to a friend describing life in the trenches' to 'Write an expository essay describing the major causes of the First World War'.

The Writing Revolution worked incredibly well at Literacy High. The students didn't only get better at writing; they got better at every subject. Why was that? Because analytical writing is the foundation skill upon which other skills are built. Improving analytical writing allowed the students at Literacy High to improve in Maths, Science, Humanities, and many other subjects besides.

CHAPTER EIGHTEEN

CASE STUDY 2:
SALSA DAYS

Not content with the success of the Writing Revolution, however, school leaders at Literacy High introduced 'Salsa Days', a new approach to speaking and listening...

Literacy High decided to focus systematically on speaking and listening across the curriculum as a means of improving literacy. Teachers realised that students at Literacy High were not as confident or indeed as articulate in speaking and listening as they were in writing. This lack of confidence was hindering their progress across the curriculum.

Accordingly, Literacy High planned whole-school activity days focused on speaking and listening, known as Salsa Days (speaking and listening secures achievement). These days helped raise the profile of speaking and listening and its role in learning.

The purpose of Salsa Days was for all teachers, irrespective of subject specialism, to explicitly teach speaking and listening skills in their subject area. The aim was to give students the confidence to articulate their views in a range of contexts.

There was a Salsa Day every term. On these days, teachers did not ask students to write within lessons; instead, all lessons were structured around speaking and listening activities. The aim was for talk to be promoted in all lessons by all subject teachers and for it to be the main focus for the day's learning. The first day focused on group discussion; the second on presenting; the third on role play; and the fourth on debating. The literacy coordinator talked to all the subject leaders about the key skills that they thought students would need. They also discussed some ground rules and emphasised the need for teachers to model effective talk.

Here is a flavour of some of the activities that took place on Literacy High's first Salsa Day:

In English, students gave speeches using a range of rhetorical devices they'd studied from famous speeches, and recited poetry.

In Maths, students carried out research and presented their findings to the rest of the class.

In History, students gave presentations on the effects of war, making use of visual aids such as maps, images and word banks.

In Citizenship, students gave presentations arguing for or against animal testing, evaluated each other's work, and voted on the best presentation.

In Drama, students performed scenes from a short play they'd written.

The natural development from Salsa Days has been to ensure that similar speaking and listening activities are now used more regularly in 'everyday' lessons. Salsa Days generated interest and awareness from all subject areas in developing higher quality speaking and listening work.

For example, the Maths department appointed a lead teacher for literacy. The Maths department also emphasises exploration and investigation in students' learning; speaking and listening are necessary skills within this context. Teachers use starter activities such as 'talking graphs', where students use graphs on the interactive whiteboard to discuss and explore mathematical concepts.

In Science, students regularly get involved in group research activities which lead on to presentations. Group discussion and debating are now embedded in Science lessons and role play is becoming a more prominent feature.

In History, it's now common for groups of students to prepare arguments for class debates. History lessons often feature activities such as 'Just a Minute' whereby students are challenged to talk non-stop for one minute on the topic of, say, the corn laws without repetition, hesitation or deviation.

In PE, students are issued with role cards which include roles such as warm-up instructor, drill instructor, and referee. Students take leading roles throughout the lesson and then evaluate the impact of their work and the effectiveness of the language they used at the end of the lesson.

This approach extends to homework, too. Often, students are set a research task to complete at home and are then asked to present their findings in class. This ensures that speaking and listening are at the heart of students' investigative learning. This only works because teachers now think carefully about how to structure and promote classroom talk such as debates, presentations, role play, and group work, and because teachers now understand the importance of explicitly teaching the speaking and listening skills required.

Speaking and listening is also embedded in extra-curricular activities at Literacy High. For example, there is a debating society, a student council which works hard to help council members learn the skills required to work together, listen to each other, make decisions, solve problems, and explain clearly what they have done.

So is it working? Teachers at Literacy High say that students appear to be more confident and self-assured than they used to be and this is reflected in their improving performance in debating competitions. A speaking and listening moderator for the speaking and listening element of GCSE English has also spoken positively of students' abilities in this area.

There has been an improving trend in the last three years in students' average points scores across all subjects as well as in the percentage of students achieving five A* to C grades. The proportion of students making expected progress in English is also above average.

CHAPTER NINETEEN

CASE STUDY 3:
THE 3LS
LEADERSHIP, LEARNING, LITERACY

Following the success of the Writing Revolution and Salsa Days, Literacy High has now begun focusing on the use of students and the wider community to promote and lead on literacy development.

Literacy High's new approach to raising standards in literacy is informed by research which shows a school can make significant learning gains when it is committed to student leadership and works hard to engage every part of the school community.

Literacy High's aim is to create a 'literacy community': in other words, a culture in which every part of the school community - and this includes parents, local primary schools, and the wider community - is affected by and contributes towards the promotion of literacy skills.

As such, the school has created a team of literacy leaders - students who assume responsibility for developing literacy across the curriculum. Students can be literacy leaders in a number of ways. They can, for example, help teachers in the classroom by identifying and making use of literacy resources. They can create their own resources to be used in the classroom. And they can teach aspects of literacy to their own class or other students.

Everything the literacy leaders produce is stored online in a shared folder and can be used by every teacher in every subject.

Eventually, Literacy High intends for every class to have at least one literacy leader and for it to be common practice for teachers to discuss ways of supporting learning with their class's literacy leader.

The literacy leaders form a group which meets regularly to discuss and support the school's literacy development. For example, they have already met to review Literacy High's marking policy. As a result, the school shortened and simplified their policy. The group have also delivered training to other teachers and students on cross-curricular literacy and have started a debating society. The society is now well-attended and has attracted guest speakers such as the local MP.

Literacy leaders begin work early...

Each day at Literacy High starts with a staff briefing but this is not the usual information exchange you might expect. Instead, literacy leaders give presentations to staff. For example, a group of students recently presented slides about reading and the importance of reading.

Following the briefing, during tutor time, literacy leaders from Years 12 and 13, as well as some volunteer parents and local people, work with Year 8 students in the library. Rather than providing support with reading as you might expect, the sixth form literacy leaders act as functional skills tutors. They provide intensive support each term to selected Key Stage 3 students with an emphasis on developing students' writing. The Year 8 students who are selected are not the weakest writers in the year group; they are students who would not otherwise receive individual support such as through the Pupil Premium or the catch-up premium.

During the sessions, the sixth form students and their Year 8 tutees work together in groups in order to plan and write a story for primary school children. The sixth form students ask the Year 8s questions to prompt their thinking. Once the stories are finished, the sixth form students work with the Year 8 students on another writing task, such as producing a script for a play to perform to Year 6 during their transition day.

As mentioned above, Literacy High's functional skills tutors consist of parents and local people as well as sixth form students. Parents and locals receive training to help them carry out their tutorship and all parents are provided with advice on how to help their children improve their literacy skills at home. Parents are also able to access the online resources folder set up by literacy leaders.

CHAPTER TWENTY

CASE STUDY 4:
READING FOR LIFE

Literacy High prides itself on being a 'reading school' which places a premium on reading for pleasure.

The library is a busy, exciting place to be and it is a resource teachers can and do want to make good use of. The library combines traditional books with electronic media.

The school runs a daily 'reading time' session (called 15 to 1) whereby students read individually for 15 minutes, which is supported by regular active reading sessions run by tutors in which students are offered support if they need it and in which students talk about what they're reading. Every class is given a book box by the library. There is a reading breakfast where students and staff can start their day in the library with refreshments and their favourite book. Competitions such as 'design a poster or bookmark' take place frequently and book vouchers are given as prizes. There is often a reading-related competition in tutor time. Various book-related events - such as World Book Day, National Poetry Day, National Storytelling Week, and Roald Dahl Day - are celebrated in style.

Reading is promoted and supported in very subject, not just English. For example, History teachers explicitly teach skimming and scanning skills and in Drama students are encouraged to read for emphasis.

CHAPTER TWENTY-ONE

CASE STUDY 5:
WRITING FOR LIFE

We've already seen how Literacy High's band of literacy leaders support some students in developing writing skills but it doesn't stop there...

To create a writing culture, Literacy High started by training its staff to improve the quality of their own writing so that they felt more confident in their teaching and their ability to provide effective feedback through marking. Then every department reviewed its schemes of work in order to identify opportunities to provide relevant contexts for extended writing.

The literacy coordinator ran an extended writing project with the Art, Science, Music and Drama departments. The effectiveness of this project subsequently made it much easier to engage teachers from other departments. The aim of the project was to gain teachers' trust by dealing head-on with the question 'What's in it for me?' Departments were asked to consider: 'What do students need to do to be able to write effectively in my subject?' Departments were then asked to describe the teaching they'd need to offer in order to support effective writing in their subject.

Having identified suitable extended writing tasks for students, departments developed a sequence of lessons for teaching writing.

To 'sell' the idea of teaching writing to teachers, it was made explicit that literacy supports learning because students need vocabulary, expression, and control over their use of language in order to meet the demands of all curriculum subjects, and literacy also helps to improve self-esteem, motivation and behaviour. Writing, in particular, helps students to sustain and order their thoughts. Ultimately, better literacy raises students' attainment in all subjects.

The project involved the following activities:

1. Teachers met collectively to share examples of good practice in extended writing and the English department gave presentations on different types of writing and the basic rules of grammar.

2. Teachers met within departments to write a teaching sequence for a piece of extended writing and to agree which key words to display within their subject. Departments also identified common errors of spelling and grammar in students' work that they wished to highlight and correct.

3. The literacy co-ordinator produced lists of common spelling mistakes for all teachers. The English department also made available lists of spellings grouped according to particular linguistic structures, such as words with unstressed vowels or double consonants. The school agreed a new literacy marking policy which was heavily influenced by the student literacy leaders.

4. Departments ensured that all their schemes of work included opportunities for extended writing.

Here are a few examples of the kinds of extended writing that took place across the curriculum in the first phase of the project:

1. In ICT, students evaluated a website.

2. In PE, students wrote a newspaper article about hosting the Olympics.

3. In Geography, students researched a country and wrote about the effects the climate and landscape had on the people who lived there.

4. In Design and Technology, students wrote about the environmental impact of supermarkets giving away plastic carrier bags.

5. In History, students wrote an essay about how the Nazis came to gain and retain power in Germany.

Many departments have changed their approach to writing tasks. For example, the Humanities department now discuss how writing will contribute to students' learning and explain why writing is important. As a result, students regard writing as the culmination or expression of their learning in Humanities.

Literacy High now provides in-class writing support for some departments. For example, an English teacher now works with the Art department in certain lessons, raising the profile of English and ensuring better quality writing.

As a result of all these actions, extended writing in every subject now has a clear sense of purpose and audience.

Whenever a visitor gives a talk in school, there is an expectation that students will respond by producing a piece of extended writing. For example, an Olympic gold medallist recently gave a talk in PE and students then wrote about their own 'Olympic Medal Moments'. The writing that results from such events is always published in an anthology which is distributed to students and parents.

CHAPTER TWENTY-TWO

CASE STUDY 6:
THE SKILLS CURRICULUM

Literacy High has a higher than average proportion of students with special educational needs. Standards in English are below average on entry. The school has developed a variety of approaches to help students develop literacy skills such as changes to the Key Stage 3 curriculum and intensive one-to-one intervention.

Another way the school is supporting Year 7 students is through the introduction of a skills-based curriculum - the intention being that students develop the skills they need in order to access knowledge.

The impact is clear: students have become much more independent and resilient, and have better communication and team-working skills. They are also better equipped to use their skills in a range of different contexts.

In each skills unit, students research a topic from a range of different sources in order to develop reading and note-taking skills. They use skimming, scanning, and reading for meaning in order to understand, evaluate and compare different primary and secondary sources. They prepare information for a particular audience, considering the most effective way to present their findings. They develop active listening and note-taking skills by listening to audio and watching video in order to gather further information, and transform their notes into an extended piece of writing – such as a letter or an essay. They practise team-work skills by presenting information in groups.

A couple of times a week, morning tutor time focuses on developing students' reading, writing and communication skills. Each week there is a different theme or topic, such as vivisection and democracy. The topics are discussed in class so the teacher can model discussion and debating skills.

CHAPTER TWENTY-THREE

CASE STUDY 7:
THE EAL CURRICULUM

Students at Literacy High are from ethnically and culturally diverse backgrounds. Many have limited English skills. The school sees confidence-building and immersion in the school culture as the priorities for those arriving into Year 7 with a limited knowledge of English. The assessment on entry of Year 7 students informs teachers of students' current levels of language acquisition, how long they have been in the British education system, if at all, and what kind of experience that has been for them.

Teachers in all departments are acutely aware of the demands placed on students by having to learn the language in which they are now being taught as well as having to acquire new subject content.

All teachers understand that some students may be reluctant to speak, read, or write in some subjects but not in others, depending on how familiar they are with the lesson content.

The Year 7 transition programme lasts a full term for those new to the English language. It provides opportunities for students to build up their basic skills as well as to develop their confidence. Transition introduces students to key concepts and vocabulary. Initially, students are also encouraged to feel comfortable using their own language to express their thoughts and ideas if they cannot confidently communicate in English.

Visual cues are often used in order to help students understand new information.

Strategies known to be effective in primary schools are adapted to support students in these early stages of language acquisition, such as prompt cards. For example, a card might say 'What might you see/hear/think? How do you know this is the first/next/last paragraph?' The purpose of prompt cards is to encourage students' development of appropriate vocabulary.

To help students who are new to the English language develop their speaking and listening skills, teachers plan 'talk' into all lessons, ensuring that discussions engage students, and that they are purposeful and structured. Teachers also encourage students to draw on their own experiences and to use their own language if they are struggling to convey an idea or feeling in English. Students are given 'wait time' in order to rehearse their contributions, so that they feel less apprehensive. Teachers introduce key vocabulary in a systematic manner. And teachers model good speaking and listening, demonstrating high expectations for all.

To help students who are new to the English language develop their writing skills, teachers provide a structure to enable students to plan their writing. Teachers also explicitly teach key words and phrases, ensuring students build up a bank of vocabulary. As above, teachers reassure students that they can write in their own language at first.

Some other features of Literacy High's work:

- Students in lessons always speak in sentences
- There is a consistent policy on marking and feedback
- There's always a book on every table
- Teachers in all subjects routinely model writing for their students
- Students are explicitly taught to organise their extended writing into well-structured paragraphs
- Marking in all subjects has a literacy focus, as do success criteria and learning objectives
- Students read individually each day for 15 minutes - this is monitored by the librarians and not confined to English lessons
- The library's role is vital and this is reflected in its budget and the quality of its staff
- The library is well-stocked with up-to-date resources and is open for breakfast each morning
- The librarian is a middle leader with real decision-making powers
- Students make good use of the library to carry out research, complete homework, and read the news
- All Year 7 and 8 students have a weekly timetabled lesson in the library where reading and research skills are explicitly taught
- Students' progress in reading is regularly tracked, and those not making sufficient progress are given extra support

PART SEVEN

RESOURCES

CHAPTER TWENTY-FOUR

ACCURACY CHECKLIST

This is a handy checklist to give to students - perhaps on a bookmark - to help them self-assess work for SPaG before they, a peer, and you mark it for content and style.

- I have divided my work into sentences separated by full stops.
- I have used capital letters at the beginning of sentences.
- I have started a new paragraph when the time, place, or subject changes.
- I have put speech marks round the words people say.
- I have started a new line for each speaker.
- I haven't missed out any words.
- I have spelt words correctly.
- I have not started all my sentences in the same way.
- I have used description which appeals to the 5 senses.

CHAPTER TWENTY-FIVE

COMMONLY CONFUSED WORDS

advice or advise?
Advice is a noun; advise is a verb
I'd like to *advise* you against it though I doubt you'll listen to my *advice*.

affect or effect?
Affect is a verb which means 'to change something'; effect is a noun which means 'the result of a change' and 'to make something happen'.

allusion or illusion?
Allusion is to make reference to something; an illusion is an imagined version of the truth.

canvas or canvass?
Canvas is a material painters use; canvass is to ask people for their opinions.

cite, site or sight?
Cite means 'to quote'; site is a place; sight is something you see.

council or counsel?
a council is a group of people elected to make decisions; counsel means 'advice' and is also a name for a lawyer.

curb or kerb?
Curb is to hold something back; a kerb is the edge of a pavement.

desert or dessert?
Desert is an arid place and also means 'to abandon'; dessert is a pudding.

disinterested or uninterested?
Disinterested means 'not taking sides'; uninterested means 'bored'.

have or of?
Though it's a common mistake, the words 'would', 'should' or 'could' are never followed by 'of' (as in could of); they can be followed by 'have'. The confusion arises from the way the contracted version sounds ('could've' sounds like 'could of').

its or it's?
Its means belonging to it; it's is short for it is.

lead or led?
Lead can be pronounced in one of two ways. When it rhymes with 'heed' it means to be in front of something. When it rhymes with 'bed' it means a heavy metal. Led is the past tense of lead (rhyming with 'heed'): "He was led out by the bouncers."

license or licence?
License is a verb; licence is a noun.
Can you license my car for me and put the licence through the letter box.

may or might?
May means things are still possible; might means they are very unlikely.

practise or practice?
Practise is a verb; practice is a noun.

I practise medicine at the local GPs' practice.

stationary or stationery?
Stationary is an adjective meaning 'standing still'; stationery is a collective noun for paper, pens, etc.

their, they're or there?
Their means 'belonging to them'; they're is short for 'they are'; there is a place, often contrasted with here.

were, we're or where
Were is the past tense of 'are'; we're is short for 'we are', and where means 'in what place'.

CHAPTER TWENTY-SIX

COMMONLY MIS-SPELT WORDS

A
accommodation
actually
alcohol
although
analyse/analysis
argument
assessment
atmosphere
audible
audience
autumn

B
beautiful
beginning
believe
beneath

buried
business

C
caught
chocolate
climb
column
concentration

D
daughter
decide/decision
definite
design
development
diamond
diary
disappear
disappoint

E
embarrass
energy
engagement
enquire
environment
evaluation
evidence
explanation

F
February
fierce
forty

fulfil
furthermore

G
guard

H
happened
health
height

I
imaginary
improvise
industrial
interesting
interrupt
issue

J
jealous

K
knowledge

L
listening
lonely
lovely

M
marriage

material
meanwhile
miscellaneous
mischief
modern
moreover
murmur

N
necessary
nervous

O
original
outrageous

P
performance
permanent
persuade/persuasion
physical
possession
potential
preparation
prioritise
process
proportion
proposition

Q
questionnaire
queue

R

reaction
receive
reference
relief
remember
research
resources

S
sincerely
skilful
soldier
stomach
straight
strategy
strength
success
surely
surprise
survey
safety
Saturday
secondary
separate
sequence
shoulder

T
technique
technology
texture
tomorrow

U
unfortunately

W
Wednesday
weight
weird
women

CHAPTER TWENTY-SEVEN

SUBJECT SPELLING LISTS

Art

abstract
easel
kiln
acrylic
exhibition
landscape
charcoal
foreground
palette
collage
frieze
pastel

collection
gallery
perspective
colour
highlight
portrait
crosshatch
illusion
sketch
dimension
impasto
spectrum
display

Design and Technology

aesthetic
hygiene
presentation
brief
ingredient
production
carbohydrate
innovation
protein
component
knife/knives
recipe
design
linen
sew
diet
machine
specification
disassemble
manufacture
technology
evaluation
mineral
tension
fabric
natural
textile
fibre
nutrition
vitamin
flour
polyester
flowchart
portfolio

English

advertise/advertisement
figurative
preposition
alliteration
genre
resolution
apostrophe
grammar
rhyme
atmosphere
imagery
scene
chorus
metaphor
simile
clause
myth
soliloquy
cliché

narrative/narrator
subordinate
comma
onomatopoeia
suffix
comparison
pamphlet
synonym
conjunction
paragraph
tabloid
consonant
personification
vocabulary
dialogue
playwright
vowel
exclamation
plural
expression
prefix

Geography

abroad
function
poverty
amenity
globe
provision
atlas
habitat
region/regional
authority
infrastructure
rural
climate
international
settlement
contour
landscape
situation
country
latitude
tourist/tourism
county
location
transport/transportation
desert
longitude
urban
employment
nation/national
wealth
erosion
physical
weather
estuary
pollution

History

agriculture/agricultural
defence
politics/political
bias
disease
priest
castle
document
propaganda
cathedral
dynasty
Protestant
Catholic
economy/economic(al)
rebel/rebellion
chronology/chronological
emigration
reign
citizen

government
religious
civilisation
immigrant
republic
colony/colonisation
imperial/imperialism
revolt/revolution
conflict
independence
siege
constitution/constitutional
invasion
source
contradict/contradiction
motive
trade
current
parliament
traitor

ICT

binary
hardware
network
byte
icon
output
cable
input
password
cartridge
interactive
preview
CD-ROM
interface
processor
computer
Internet
program
connect/connection

justify
scanner
cursor
keyboard
sensor
data/database
megabyte
server
delete
memory
software
disk
modem
spreadsheet
document
module
virus
electronic
monitor
graphic
multimedia

Library

alphabet/alphabetical
encyclopaedia
novel
anthology
extract
photocopy
article
fantasy
publisher
author
genre
relevant/relevance
catalogue
glossary
romance
classification
index
section
content
irrelevant/irrelevance
series
copyright
librarian
system
dictionary
magazine
thesaurus
editor
non-fiction

Mathematics

addition
estimate
positive
adjacent
equation
quadrilateral
alternate
fraction
questionnaire
angle
graph
radius
amount
guess
ratio
approximately
horizontal
recurring
average
isosceles
reflect/reflection
axis/axes
kilogram
regular/irregular
calculate
kilometre
rhombus
centimetre
litre

rotate/rotation
circumference
measure
square
corresponding
metre
subtraction
co-ordinate
minus
symmetry/symmetrical
decimal
multiply/multiplication
triangle/triangular
degree
parallel/parallelogram
tonne
denominator
negative
vertex/vertices
diameter
numerator
vertical
digit
percentage
volume
divide/division
perimeter
weight
equilateral
perpendicular

Music

choir
minim
score
chord
minor
semibreve
chromatic
musician
synchronise
composition/conductor
octave
syncopation
crotchet
orchestra/orchestral
tempo
dynamics
ostinato
ternary
harmony
percussion
timbre
instrument/instrumental
pitch
triad
interval
quaver
vocal
lyric
rhythm
major
scale

PE

active/activity
injury
qualify
agile/agility
league
relay
athletic/athlete
medicine
squad
bicep
mobile/mobility
tactic
exercise
muscle
tournament
field
personal
triceps
gym/gymnastic
pitch
hamstring
quadriceps

PSHE

able/ability
effort
reality
achieve/achievement
emotion/emotional
relationship
addict/addiction
encourage/encouragement
represent/representative
approve/approval
gender
reward
communication
generous/generosity
sanction
control
involve/involvement
sexism/sexist
dependant/dependency
prefer/preference
stereotype
discipline
pressure
discussion
racism/racist

RE

baptism
Hindu/Hinduism
prophet
Bible/biblical
hymn
religious/religion
Buddhist/Buddhism
immoral/immorality
shrine
burial
Islam
sign
celebrate/celebration
Israel
Sikh/Sikhism
ceremony
Judaism/Jewish
special
Christian
marriage

spirit/spiritual
commandment
miracle
symbol
commitment
moral/morality
synagogue
creation
Muslim
temple
disciple
parable
wedding
faith
pilgrim/pilgrimage
worship
festival
pray/prayer
funeral
prejudice

Science

absorb
exchange
organism
acid
freeze
oxygen
alkaline
frequency
particles
amphibian
friction
predator
apparatus
function
pressure
chemical
growth
reproduce

circulate/circulation
hazard
respire/respiration
combustion
insect
solution
condensation
laboratory
temperature
cycle
liquid
thermometer
digest/digestion
mammal
vertebrate
element
method
vessel
evaporation
nutrient

CHAPTER TWENTY-EIGHT

STEM WORDS FOR LEARNING OBJECTIVES

Below are some stem words, modelled on Bloom's taxonomy, which you could use to frame learning objectives...

Knowledge:
Arrange
Define
Describe
List
Match
Memorise
Name
Order
Quote
Recognise
Recall
Repeat
Reproduce

Suggested activities:
Make a timeline of events.
List all the facts.
Write a list of...
Draw a chart showing...
Make an acrostic.
Recite a poem.

Comprehension:
Characterise
Classify
Complete
Describe
Discuss
Explain
Identify
Illustrate
Recognise
Report
Sort
Translate

Suggested activities:
Draw a picture to show...
Make a cartoon strip showing the sequence of events.
Write and perform a play based on the story.
Retell the story in your words.
Write a summary report of the event.
Create a flow chart to illustrate the sequence of events.

Application:
Apply
Calculate
Choose
Demonstrate
Dramatise
Interpret
Operate
Perform
Practise

Role-Play
Sketch
Solve
Suggest

Suggested activities:
Construct a model to demonstrate how it will work.
Make a scrapbook about the areas of study.
Take a collection of photographs to demonstrate the main topic.
Make up a puzzle game using the ideas from the text.
Design an appropriate costume for the era depicted in the text.
Write a textbook about...
Design a marketing strategy for your product.

Analysis:
Analyse
Appraise
Categorise
Compare
Contrast
Differentiate
Distinguish
Examine
Explore
Investigate
Question
Research
Test

Suggested activities:
Design a questionnaire to gather further information.
Write a commercial to sell a new product.
Conduct an investigation to produce information to support your point of view.
Make a flow chart to show the critical stages outlined in the text.
Construct a graph to illustrate the main trends.
Make a family tree showing the main characters' relationships to each other.
Put on a play.
Write a biography of the main character.

Prepare a report.
Review a work of art in terms of form, colour and texture.

Synthesis:
Combine
Compose
Construct
Create
Devise
Design
Formulate
Hypothesise
Integrate
Merge
Organise
Plan
Propose
Synthesise

Suggested activities:
Invent a machine to...
Design a building for...
Create a new product.
Describe your feelings about...
Write a TV show, play, short role play, song or monologue about...
Design a record, book, or magazine cover for...
Design an advert to sell...

Evaluation:
Appraise
Argue
Assess
Critique
Evaluate
Examine
Inspect
Judge
Justify
Rank

Rate
Review

Suggested activities:
Prepare a list of criteria to judge...
Prioritise... according to...
Conduct a debate about...
Make a booklet outlining 5 things you regard as important about...
Form a panel to discuss your views about...
Write a letter to ... advising on...
Write an annual report on...
Prepare a case about...

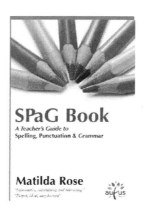

SPaG Book
A Teacher's Guide to
Spelling, Punctuation & Grammar

Matilda Rose
"Informative, entertaining and interesting."
"Perfect, ideal, easy-to-read."

aurus

CHAPTER TWENTY-NINE

FREE GIFT!

SPaG BOOK
A coffee break synopsis

What is grammar?

Grammar is a combination of:

Syntax: the study of sentence structure, an analysis of main and subordinate clauses, of simple, compound and complex sentences, of subjects, verbs and objects, and so on;

Morphology: the study of word structure, an analysis of stem (or root) words, of prefixes and suffixes, inflections for tense, number and person, and so on;

Semantics: the study of meaning, an analysis of the things, people, and events we refer to when we're talking, as well as how meanings - both literal (denotation) and implied (connotation) - are conveyed, and how words can mask their true meaning (e.g. through the use of euphemism).

What aspects of grammar should be taught in school?

Grammar teaching must include the linguistic structures of <u>words</u>, <u>sentences</u> and whole <u>texts,</u> and must cover:
- the word classes (or parts of speech) and their grammatical functions;
- the structure of phrases and clauses and how they can be combined (by coordination and subordination) to make complex sentences;
- paragraph structure and how to form different types of paragraph;
- the structure of whole texts, including cohesion, and the conventions of openings and conclusions in different types of writing; and
- the use of appropriate grammatical terminology in order to reflect on the meaning and clarity of both spoken and written language.

Why do we need to teach SPaG?

According to the National Literacy Strategy, the only explicit justification for teaching grammar is its contribution to writing skills. Grammar teaching, the theory goes, promotes students' understanding and helps them to know, notice, discuss and explore language features. The quality of students' writing is also affected by their motivation, creativity and insight, all of which may also be improved by grammar teaching. Grammar teaching may also provide a tool for learning other languages.

How should we teach SPaG?

Grammar teaching works best when it is:
- placed in context
- made relevant to students' writing
- made explicit as well as taught through investigations
- revisited systematically
- taught across the curriculum not confined to English lessons

Why is SPaG important now?

SPaG is now tested at the end of Key Stage 2. The new SPaG tests assess elements of the current English curriculum including:
- sentence grammar (through identification and grammatical accuracy);
- punctuation (through identification and grammatical accuracy);
- vocabulary (through grammatical accuracy); and
- spelling.

SPaG is also part of the assessment criteria of four GCSE subjects: English literature, history, geography, and religious studies, where it accounts for 5% of the final mark. SPaG at GCSE is about:
- accurate spelling;
- effective use of punctuation to ensure clarity and to aid meaning;
- consistently obeying the rules of grammar; and
- effective use of a wide range of specialist (by which is meant 'subject specific') vocabulary.

Isn't SPaG an English teacher's job?

Yes and no. The National Curriculum and Ofsted say all teachers should view themselves as teachers of literacy, regardless of their subject specialism. Also, teaching literacy is *not* the same as teaching English. Literacy is about helping students to access the whole curriculum. Literacy is about helping students to read subject information and helping students to write in order that they can assimilate that information and then demonstrate their learning.

Teaching literacy might take the form of:

- displaying key words;
- writing three key words for each lesson on the white board at the start of the lesson and reinforcing the meaning and usage of these words throughout the lesson;
- giving students the opportunity to say key words out loud,

then asking them to write a sentence using the word in context;
- giving students the opportunity to repeat a new skill;
- providing students with workbooks to record new vocabulary – like a personal subject dictionary;
- providing cut-up sentences on a subject-specific topic and asking students to reconstruct them;
- analysing the audience, purpose and style of the texts being studied;
- providing opportunities for group discussion and debate, reinforcing the rules of effective group talk.

The history of English

English is very, very old and doesn't make much sense. But it's better than French.

The building blocks of English

It's wise to study English in its component parts starting with:

Letters, of which there are 26, 20 consonants, 5 vowels and 'y' which can be either
which make

Phonemes (units of sound) **and morphemes** (units of meaning like prefixes and suffixes)
which make

Words (like nouns, verbs, adjectives and adverbs, connectives, pronouns, determiners, and prepositions)
which make

Phrases
which make

Clauses (a main clause makes sense on its own because it has a verb, a subordinate clause doesn't)
which make

Sentences, of which there are three main types: simple (subject-verb-object), compound (two or more main clauses joined by connective words), and complex (with at least one main and one subordinate clause). And four main functions: declarative (statements), imperative (commands), interrogative (questions), and exclamative (exclaiming something)
which make

Paragraphs, which might helpfully start with an adverb such as 'firstly', and which are instigated each time a new point is made, whenever there's a time shift or for dramatic effect
which make

Texts, like this book which I hope you have enjoyed and found of good use. Thank you for reading it. Happy SPaG-ing.

REFERENCES AND BIBLIOGRAPHY

Allen, J; *Words, words, words: Teaching vocabulary in grades 4–12*; Stenhouse Publishers; 1999

Armbruster, .B. B. & Lehr, F. & Osborn, J; *Put reading first: The research building blocks of reading instruction (2nd ed.)* in National Institute for Literacy; 2003

Assessment Reform Group; *Assessment for Learning: Ten Principles*; from www.assessment-reform-group.org.uk; 2002

Beck, I.L. & McKeown, M.G; *Increasing young low-income children's oral vocabulary repertoires through rich and focused instruction* in The Elementary School Journal, 107, 251–271; 2007

Beck, I.L. & McKeown, M.G. & Kucan, L; *Bringing words to life: Robust vocabulary instruction;* Guilford Press; 2002; New York

Beck, I. & McKeown, M.G. & Kucan, L.; *Creating robust vocabulary: Frequently asked questions and extended examples*; Guilford Press; 2008; New York

Biemiller, A; *Words worth teaching: Closing the vocabulary gap*; McGraw-Hill; 2010

Black, P & Wiliam, D; 'Assessment and classroom learning' from *Assessment in Education 5*; 1998

Black, P & Wiliam, D; *Inside the Black Box: Raising Standards Through Classroom Assessment*; London School of Education, King's College; 1998; London

Black, P et al; *Assessment for Learning: Putting it into Practice*; Open University Press; 2003; Maidenhead

Bromley, M J; *A Teacher's Guide To Outstanding Lessons & Assessment for Learning;* Autus Books, England; 2012

Bromley, M J; *Ofsted: Thriving Not Surviving;* Autus Books, England; 3rd edition 2014

Bromley, M J; *Teach!;* Autus Books, England; 2014

Brownlie, F; Close, S; Wingren, L; *Reaching for Higher Thought*; Cold Spring Harbor Laboratory Press; 1988

Catts et al's (2002) research is cited in many papers including a Longitudinal Study from University of Iowa www.uiowa.edu

De Bono, E; in O'Sullivan; *Questions Worth Asking*; Brighton and Hove LEA; 2003; Brighton

Department for Education; *The National Literacy Strategy: Framework for Teaching*; DfEE (as was); 1998; London

Dweck, C; 'Motivational processes affecting learning' from *American Psychologist 41*; 1986

Elstgeest, J; 'The right questions at the right time' from Harlen, W (ed) *Taking the Plunge: How to Teach Science More Effectively*; Heinemann; 1985

Fernald, A. & Perfors, A.& Marchman, V.A; *Picking up speed in understanding: Speech processing efficiency and vocabulary growth across the 2nd year* in Developmental Psychology, 42(1), 98–116; 2006

Fleer, M. & B. Raban; *Literacy and Numeracy that counts from birth to five years: a review of the literature* from DEST Early Childhood learning resources; 2005

Gavelek et al.; *Integrated literacy instruction* in M.L. Kamil, P.B. Mosenthal, P.D. Pearson, & R. Barr (Eds.); 2000

Graham, L. & Wong, B.Y.L; *Comparing two modes of teaching question-answering strategy for enhancing reading comprehension: Didactic and self-instructional training* in Journal of Learning Disabilities, 26, 270–279; 1993

Harvey, S & Goudvis A; *Strategies that Work: Teaching Comprehension for Understanding and Engagement*; Stenhouse Publishers; 2003

Hirsch, ED; *The Schools We Need*; Anchor Press; 1999

Johnson, D & Johnson, R; *Learning Together and Alone* from Cooperative Learning www.co-operation.org; 1999

Keene, E & Zimmerman S; *Mosaic of Thought, The Power of Comprehension Strategy Instruction*; Heinemann; 2007

Knight, S; *Questions: Assessing and Developing Students' Understanding and Thinking in Literacy*; Manchester School Improvement Service; 2000

Lewis, M & Wray, D; *Implementing Effective Literacy Initiatives in the Secondary School* in Education Studies Vol. 27, No. 1; University of Warwick; 2001

Marshall, B & Wiliam, D; *English Inside the Black Box*; King's College London, 2006, London

Morgan, N & Saxton, J; *Asking Better Questions*; Pembroke Publishers, 2006, Ontario, Canada

Morrow, L.M. & Strickland, D. S. & Wood, D. G; *Literacy instruction in half- and whole-day kindergarten*; National Early Literacy Panel, 1998

Myhill, D & Fisher, R; *Using Talk to Support Writing*; SAGE Publications; 2010

Ofsted: *Improving Literacy in Secondary Schools*; from www.ofsted.gov.uk HMSO; 2013; London

Ofsted; *Good Assessment in Secondary Schools*; from www.dfe.gov.uk HMSO; 2003; London

Ofsted; *Moving English Forward*; from www.oftsed.gov.uk HMSO; 2012; London

Ofsted; *Removing Barriers to Literacy*; from www.ofted.gov.uk, HMSO; 2011; London

Pressley, M., & Mohan, l. & Raphael, L.M. & Fingeret, L; *How does Bennet Woods Elementary School produce such high reading and writing achievement?* in Journal of Educational Psychology, 99(2), 221–240; 2007

Rigney, D; *The Matthew Effect*; Columbia University Press; 2010

Rinaldi, L. & Sells, D. & McLaughlin, T.F; *The effects of reading racetracks on sight word acquisition of elementary students* in Journal of Behavioural Education, 7, 219–234; 1997

Rose, M; *SPaG Book: A Teacher's Guide to Spelling, Punctuation, and Grammar;* Autus Books, England; 2013

Rowe, M B; 'Relation of wait-time and rewards to the development of language, logic and fate control' from *Journal of Research in Science Teaching 11*; High Scope; 1995

Sampson, G; *English for the English: A Chapter on National Education*; Cambridge University Press; 1975

Sinek, S; *Start with Why*; Penguin; 2009; London

Skeat, J. & Green, J. & Wood, P & B. Laidlaw; *Speech and Language in The Early Years: A nested study of the Linking Schools and Early Years project*; Melbourne Royal Children's Hospital Education Institute; 2010

Sparks, A & Reese, E & Leyva D; *A review of parent interventions for preschool children's language and emergent literacy* in Journal of Early Childhood Literacy 10, 97-117; SAGE publications; 2010

Stevenson, H W & Stigler, J W; *The Learning Gap*; Simon & Schuster; 1992

Stigler, J W & Hiebert, J; *The Teaching Gap*; Simon & Schuster; 1999

Suffolk LEA; from www.slamnet.org.uk

Tomopolous, S. & Dreyer, B. & Tamis-LeMonda, C. & Flynn, V. & Rovira, I. & Tineo, W. & Mendelsohn, A; *Books, toys, parent–child interaction and development* in young Latino children in Ambulatory Pediatics, 6(2), 72–78; 2006

Vygotsky, L; *Thinking and Speaking*; MIT Press; 1934

Willingham, D; *Why Don't Students Like School?;* Jossey Bass; 2010

Youngs, B B; *The Six Vital Ingredients of Self-Esteem*; from Dryden G & Boss, J

All the National Literacy Trust publications cited in this book, including *Children's and Young People's Reading* (2012) and *Literacy: State of the Nation* (2012) are available from www.literacytrust.org.uk

ABOUT THE AUTHOR

Matilda Rose is a teacher and writer based in the UK.

You can follow her on Twitter: @between2thorns

You can read her blog: between2thorns.wordpress.com

ALSO BY MATILDA ROSE

The Cruellest Month

SPaG Book:
A Teacher's Guide to Spelling, Punctuation, and Grammar

EDUCATION

Supporting schools and colleges in the UK

Visit www.solutionsforschool.co.uk for more information

Including:

FREE monthly teacher newsletter containing all the latest education news

FREE news and blogs service

FREE resources

High-quality, low-cost books for teachers and leaders

A range of consultancy and training services

Follow Autus on Twitter: @solution4school

AUTUS BOOKS

England, UK

www.booksforschool.eu

Twitter: @ebooksforschool

First published in 2014

Copyright © Matilda Rose 2014

ISBN-13: 978-1500646578
ISBN-10: 1500646571

Printed in Great Britain
by Amazon